Someone GETS ME

How Smart and Intensely Sensitive People Can
Thrive in an Insensitive World

Someone Gets Me

How Smart and Intensely Sensitive People Can
Thrive in an Insensitive World

Dianne A. Allen, MA

Published by: Visions Applied, LLC., Riverview, FL

Library of Congress Control Number: 2023908721

ISBN: 978-0-9995778-6-8

Cover Design by: Richard Jibaja

Printed in the United States of America.

DEDICATED TO:

All the quirky, intense people on Earth with a great mission.

I see you!

Acknowledgments

This book was inspired by the many intensely sensitive people who are thriving in an insensitive world. Some of you have found your way and others are still searching, while there are some whom we have lost. Through all of life's twists and turns, each one of you has touched my heart and soul in ways words cannot describe.

Thank you, Raymond Hinst, for suggesting I write a book for intensely sensitive people "so they have a place to turn for support and help." It has been years in the writing. Your support and encouragement have been very valuable. When I think of you, I always think *"someone gets me!"*

Many thanks to Dr. Matt Zakreski who generously wrote the foreword for this book. He is a light for many neurodiverse, intense, and sensitive people in our world. Thank you to Dr. Eric Windhorst and Sara Julian for reviewing this text and offering valuable feedback. Your input and support are deeply meaningful.

As this book came into being, several ambassadors for my work have been my cheerleaders while many others listened and shared with me as I processed and created the content. Thank you to each of you and to the countless others who support my work and vision.

Individually acknowledging the many intensely sensitive people who inspired the stories within would be too cumbersome. Each story has elements of actual people with different names and identifying information to secure their privacy. If you resonate with any of the characters, you are reminded that you are not alone. Using creative license, each story has aspects that are for illustrative purposes. No story is solely about a single person.

I acknowledge you, the reader, and your loved ones for whom this book is intended to educate, inspire, uplift and support on the road of being intensely sensitive in an insensitive world.

Finally, I wish to thank our Creator for the inspiration and gifts for this work as part of bringing my deeper soul's vision to life. My trust and faith in the greater Good remain steadfast.

CONTENTS

Introduction 14

Chapter I. 17
The Spiritual Juice – Fundamental Principles of Living

Chapter II. 32
Being Intensely Sensitive in an Insensitive World

Chapter III. 40
Creating Personal Safety

Chapter IV. 45
Making Friends with Your Intense Sensitivities

Chapter V. 73
Standing in Your Personal Authority

Chapter VI. 78
Inner Integrity

Chapter VII. 83
Opening to Possibilities

Chapter VIII. 96
Your Intrinsic Wealth

Chapter IX. 100
Allow Connection

Chapter X. 105
Release Fear, Procrastination, and Perfectionism

Chapter XI..114
Release Blocks to Thrive

Chapter XII....119
The Importance of Compassion

Chapter XIII...125
Healthy Boundaries

Chapter XIV...131
Being Your Authentic Self

Chapter XV..138
Faith, Trust, and Imagination

Chapter XVI...145
Leaving Your Legacy

Conclusion..153

Appendix 154
Are You Intensely Sensitive?
Take this Quiz and See!

Glossary of Terms 156

About the Author 158

I was always fascinated by people considered to be completely normal, because I find them the weirdest of all.

~~ Johnny Depp

FOREWORD

"Don't be nervous." "Focus." "Calm down." "Don't worry; be happy!"

I often joke with my therapy clients that if these sentences worked, I would be out of a job. Thankfully (for me as a clinical psychologist, at least) they don't. But the existence and prevalence of these phrases indicates something much deeper. All these phrases have in common a specific ideology about feelings: namely, don't have them.

I get it. Feelings can be disruptive, unpleasant, painful, and stigmatizing. But they're real! We actually hurt ourselves more by ignoring or trying to push our feelings away, rather than sitting with the feelings or expressing them. But the temptation to avoid our unpleasant feelings is strong, as is the relatively recent tendency to smother them in a heaping amount of Toxic Positivity (I.e., the #goodvibesonly crowd). The problem is that both approaches trade short-term gain for long-term pain. If we really want to be our best selves, so much of what we do has to involve feeling our feelings and letting them work for us, not against us.

My guess is that you picked up this book because someone in your life has, at some point, called you *sensitive*. Perhaps they meant it kindly. Perhaps they were mean about it. Perhaps they have even included the dreaded rider of calling you "too" sensitive. Regardless, here you are, having just opened your shopping bag or Amazon delivery box, wondering if this is the book that will finally help you to understand just what to do about being **so** sensitive.

Well, the good news is that you're in luck. The interesting news is that the solution is almost certainly not what you think it is.

Being sensitive can be a superpower. And not to go all "Uncle Ben" on you here, but with great power comes great responsibility. Ignore it, and you may wither on the vine. Give into it, and you can drown. Sensitivity is a part of us, however, and we must find a way to integrate it into our lives in a way that is authentic and consistent with our own values. The first step in that process is owning the fact that sensitivity is not a thing that we carry; it is a thing that we *are*.

One of the original definitions of sensitivity is "pertaining to the faculty of the soul that receives and analyzes sensory information" (Oxford English Dictionary, 2021). Our sensitivity is a very deep part of ourselves that clamors to be heard. It is deeply personal and wise. Yes, it isn't always pleasant or positive, but it is always important.

Often, when we look back at the thing/person/concept that we were being sensitive to, it represents an aspect of our lives that we were deeply unsatisfied with. For example, I used to feel the need to do very formal presentations, because I thought that is what a Serious Academic ® person does. And I hated talking that way! I was much more sensitive to critique and criticism when I was presenting about content that I didn't care about in a way that was not authentic to me. Now I get to do talks all over the world, and I do them my way: informally, with an emphasis on storytelling and connection. My sensitivity to the old way was trying to teach me an important lesson, but it took me a long time to hear it.

Sensitivity is always communication; the trick is becoming ready to hear those messages and make meaningful change. And while it is never too late to change (I wouldn't be much of a psychologist if I thought otherwise!), the sooner we open ourselves to that messaging, the better! Like I am fond of saying, the best time to change was five years ago; the second-best time is right now. Changing that relationship to our sensitivity can be a long and arduous process; you certainly would benefit from having an expert guide.

Enter the wonderful and fabulous Dianne Allen, the author of this amazing book and our guide to making sensitivity work for us.

Dianne Allen is one of the most authentically sensitive people I have ever met. She speaks from the heart, shoots from the hip, and cares deeply, and fiercely, about her work. The first time that I met Dianne I was being interviewed on her excellent podcast and she told me that we would be "just letting the conversation flow between us, letting the questions come to me and seeing where we end up" rather than giving me a list of questions for me to answer. Which, as an extrovert and a recovering Serious Academic speaker, I totally loved. We dove in and began trading stories and responses, facts and figures, impressions, and reactions. And as our conversation flowed, I realized two vital things.

One: Dianne *told* me that she would be letting her intuition be her guide in our interview. She didn't actually ask me if I was ok with it before diving into our conversation.

Two: I was having a blast.

That's Dianne. She trusts her own instincts and intuition so powerfully that you can feel held by her glowing confidence. And if you watch our interview, in which our shared vision grew into a two-part talk (it's on YouTube!), you'll notice how much fun that we're having. You can also note that while Dianne trusts her own instincts, she also trusts my instincts (and the other people she works with) to lead me in the right direction. There's no hand holding with Dianne. She blazes a trail and knows that your own skills can rise to her occasion.

My friends, listen to the words of this book. You will see your flaws and shortcomings and realize that they are not the final draft of your life; they are bumps on a much longer road. By owning our own struggles and, thus, our humanity, we become more human and more empathetic towards our own journey. You will also learn to trust your instincts as well, to listen to your sensitivity, and to embody words like giving, gratitude, and compassion. These are all good terms and, frankly, terms that I am sure that you have heard before. But if they haven't landed for you before, it is possible that you haven't had the right guide.

There are so many reasons that we try not to listen to our sensitivity: it can be disruptive, painful, and dysregulating. Society tells us not to listen to our sensitivity for many reasons, largely because other people often value their own comfort over our own because it's easier for them. To that, I say, "So what?" You aren't your best self if you are pushing back or fighting your own feelings. The best, baddest, coolest, most authentic version of yourself is the one that is listening to that sensitivity and making it work for you. That version of you helps the most people, does the most good, and lifts yourself up.

Dianne ends her podcasts by saying that we should face towards the sun. One of the comments on our first podcast was from a person who enjoyed what we had to say, but was waylaid by that final comment, "What," she said, "should I do if I cannot face the sun at this point of my life?" I mentioned this comment to Dianne, and she got this big "I got this" smile on her face. I knew that this woman's sensitivity had guided her to Dianne's message, and that our fabulous author's intuition would take her forward on her healing journey. I don't know what happened to that woman, but I am confident that, wherever she is, she's facing her own sun in her own way thanks in no small part to the messaging that became this book.

So, let me end by saying this, my friends. Life is hard. And if you find that you cannot face the sun, for whatever reason, then face Dianne Allen. Her words, energy, and wisdom will carry you forward until you can face the sun on your own. And when you finally do, no one will be happier for you than her.

Happy reading (and keep facing that sun!)

Matthew Zakreski, PsyD.

www.drmattzakreski.com

March 2022

INTRODUCTION

This book comes from a life of being intensely sensitive. I also excel when working with intensely sensitive people, those that other counselors and therapists would shy away from in the various centers I worked. Being gifted while also having spiritual giftedness can be empowering and dis-empowering at the same time until you come to a deep love and appreciation for your unique essence that emerges in beautiful ways that may not be understood by many. I see you. I understand your struggles, existential angst and loneliness. My goal here is to offer support, inspiration, and practical actions to support you. This book is intended to be adjunct to your other self-development activities and is not intended to stand alone as your only resource.

I am an intensely sensitive person, and my journey has taken many twists and turns. The intensity with which I experience everything seems to be more profound than many I know. As a young girl, I had no information about being sensitive so I concluded that something must be wrong with me or maybe I was an alien. As I grew, I struggled often because of being misunderstood and not really understanding myself. I remember having intense feelings and my family looking at me in won-der. I also remember being intensely focused on intellectual pursuits to the exclusion of being distracted. From an early age, people often treated me like a miniature adult, not a child. I also remember bumping into my spir-itual sensitivities with my friends. I would know things intuitively and I innocently thought they could see it or know it as well. I was wrong. I did not even know the words ``spiritual" or "intuition", yet the experience was very real. I was often judged and ridiculed by peers and adults alike leading to feelings of inferiority for many years.

My adulthood has been quite the ride as well. I find myself relat-ing to and understanding many types of people from many walks of life. Somehow, "I get them". I believe it is because of my gifts, intensities, and sensitivities. Adding years of education and knowledge to my inherent gifts has made for an interesting life. As time has unfolded, I have learned to trust my gut and my sensitivities. This has been a long, and at times, difficult road. Years of being misunderstood and judged by many helps me focus on truly understanding others. Of course, the more I understand myself, the more I understand others. I believe our inherent connection as humans offers great wisdom when we slow down and pay attention.

Being intensely sensitive and smart is not an excuse to control others, act out, or create havoc. It comes with a responsibility to use your smarts, sensitivities, and intensities for Good rather than selfish gain. There are many who use their talents for selfish gain or to harm others. I believe that is a misuse of the gifts and power bestowed upon us. Our roads can be challenging, disheartening, thrilling, blissful, and everything in between yet it is our unique responsibility to gain understanding by going within and being honest, open, and willing to grow and serve.

Now, years later, the road makes more sense. My intense sensitivities have been the root of my life's vocation and work. This gift, that has at times felt like a curse, has afforded me deep understanding with which to help others. This is clearly a blessing for me and those with whom I work. There have been great challenges and great joys along the way. My world is still intense, and my intuition and sensitivities are emerging more clearly as I release the old emotions and patterns.

Intense sensitivities can be defined simply as a unique combination of spiritual sensitivities/intuition and intensities/overexcitabilities that are common in gifted individuals. All too often the spiritual sensitivity is left out of the equation and discussion, and I firmly believe it belongs in the forefront of the discussion. The more I delve into my inner world and engage with others who are intensely sensitive, spiritual presence and power are prominent in that person's life experience. To only focus on the intellectual or emotional aspects without honoring the spiritual force makes no sense to me when looking at a human as a whole and complete being. So, when I use the term, "Intense Sensitivities" I am referring to the uniquely expressed combination of a person with intensities-overexcitabilities who also has strong spiritual sensitivities.

This book is meant to support your intense and often confusing life through story, information, and resources. I believe that you have a beautiful and unique essence that when acknowledged and given a voice, can thrive in ways that will inspire you. While I am aware it is impossible to cover every scenario, I trust you will find yourself in these pages. You are not alone.

Whether you are reading for you or a loved one, read with an open heart and an open mind. I encourage you to look for similarities that can support you and those you love. For more information about my work, visit www.visionsapplied.com.

Take the Intense Sensitivity Quiz in the back of this book. Share your results in the *Someone Gets Me* Facebook Group. *www.facebook.com/groups/someonegetsme* I will be sure to comment and encourage you.

Welcome. Enjoy.

Dianne

CHAPTER 1.

The Spiritual Juice – Fundamental Principles of Living

The secret of health for both mind and body is not to mourn for the past, nor to worry about the future, but to live the present moment wisely and earnestly.
~~ *Gautama Buddha*

Life is meant to be juicy. Juicy love deeply touches your soul because it is your essence coming forward. Compassion, Kindness, Gratitude and Giving are vital ingredients for a fulfilled and juicy life. Your spiritual juice emanates from your inner connection to Source. This chapter reminds you that your inner essence is flowing with a natural power that is meant for Good. You can witness these principles in daily life. For me, Joy is the state through which these principles emanate. I believe that Joy is our natural state and the fundamental spiritual juice that animates us. So, Joy is the base ingredient for your juice and the other flavors are available for you to add as you are inspired!

Living by fundamental principles rooted in spiritual ideas gives you a firm and secure, safe, and unwavering platform from which to live and express your gifts. By investing time each day to connect to your inner resources and enhance your expression of these principles, your success and happiness is assured. Principles that are vital include: Faith, Love, Compassion, Kindness, Regeneration, Strength, Zeal, Wisdom, Imagination, and Understanding. These principles are ever-present and seek expression through each person. In intensely sensitive people, the experience can be profound as well as tricky at times. Your spiritual sensitivities as these principles are expressed can greatly enhance your intensities. How you manage your environment reflects how you are engaging or avoiding these powerful energies that are seeking to emerge and be expressed through you.

There is beauty in your individual expression of your spiritual juice. These fundamental principles are the sweetness of life that add depth and substance to your connections. You are designed to be in authentic connection with your inner self, others and the Greater Universe. Your unique combination of spiritual principles coming alive within your personal expression as a human being is a one-of-a-kind beauty. Truly, you are a masterpiece. Any belief you have to the contrary is a misinterpretation or outright lie you picked up somewhere along the way.

Challenges occur when you become distracted by fear, grief, doubt, worry, guilt, and the like. When your attention is on something other than the Higher Principles, things can often go awry. Distractions cause many challenges including limiting your connections. Part of being an intensely sensitive person in an insensitive world is to seek inner discipline, peace, and focus while the external world moves about around you. Yes, this takes time and attention. Investing in this level of inner focus has great rewards emotionally, mentally, physically, spiritually, and socially. I invite you to make the investment in yourself. No better time to decide than now. Start wherever you are at this moment. Know that even a small 0.5% change per day yields powerful results.

Your spiritual juice is yearning to emerge and be seen. Any small opening you create will yield tangible results. The all or nothing approach is not effective and can cause a healing crisis or burnout. I suggest you decide to create an opening while being deeply honest with yourself. Then allow the Universe to support you through inspired thoughts and actions, other people, situations and events, and compelling inner guidance. The more open you are within, the more opportunity and possibilities you will see. Ask yourself about each of these principles and how they are showing up in your thoughts, words, and actions. This is a great place to discern many of your next steps.

Let's look at a few of the key principles and how they underpin the juice of your life.

KINDNESS

Just be nice! This phrase was common years ago. I still hear it today. Be kind. What does this mean exactly? "To be" is a state. It is a way of living and breathing that emanates from within and radiates outward. A state is different from a feeling or emotion. A state is a way of being and a feeling is the energy that tells you that you are alive. How you describe them helps create your experience. This should not be confused with an action that is generated from your physicality. This is where the "Just be Nice" phrase misses the true essence of being kind. Kindness emanates from your inner essence while being nice is an action. When you are "being" a particular principle, it means that it is in the inner core of you, and it is deeply woven in the fabric of your innermost self. You are acting from your inner principles rather than reacting to the outer world.

Kind is a word that has great depth and meaning. To be kind is powerful. There are specific areas that are important here. One area is being kind to others, especially the vulnerable. A kind person is gentle and caring while they assist another without any desire for future gain. The motive for their action is kindness, nothing more.

Then there is kindness within. Many people act kind at times on the outside yet their inner kindness toward self is suffering or completely neglected. Are you kind with yourself? Is your inner world of self-talk kind and supportive? When you are not so kind to you, it is hard to be authentically kind to others. Your inner world sends signals. If you are not kind inwardly and you act kind to another, you may be misunderstood or even judged as inauthentic. Whether you are aware of this or not, your energetic presence introduces you before you say or do anything. This is one of the many benefits to inner integrity and alignment. The mixed messages cause skepticism in others even if they don't know why.

Being authentic from the inside out creates an environment where your intense sensitivities can be fully honored. This is where the juice of life begins to flow with integrity and authentic presence.

Meet Jim

Jim is the oldest of four siblings raised by a loving and kind family. He is a sensitive and intelligent creative. Jim, like his siblings and parents, has many talents and gifts. He is a visionary. His challenges have come about because his visionary skills and dreams do not fit into the family vision for Jim. See, he is the oldest and he has a family tradition to live up to the expectation of the family lineage. He followed the family tradition through college then he veered off the prescribed path and began his own visionary journey. His family is supportive of Jim and his aspirations, yet they do not understand his intense sensitivities which caused some family concern and struggle within their relationships. His family wanted to support him, yet they had no reference point to understand how to support his divergent lifestyle from the way he was raised.

Jim called me and we began to work together for some time. He shared his visions and talents and gifts with me. We met with his family, and they also shared their respect for Jim even though they did not understand him and his choices. Jim's choices for his life were outside of the paradigm that he was raised under and that his family are accustomed to. This is where the work of connecting the intensely sensitive with the others came in the form of bridge building and educating all the family in a way each could understand.

Jim is a kind man and struggled with his boundaries and communication with his family and business associates. We worked through some of these concerns as we met together with the business associates and family members to work toward a greater understanding of each other's views and paradigms. Both Jim, his family, and his business associates were saying the same thing about their goals, yet they seemed to miss each other in the day-to-day experience. Jim and I worked on ways to express his kind heartedness that worked for him while maintaining his integrity to his heart's desire. He was able to understand that kindness is not weakness and that he could establish and maintain healthy boundaries and be able to remain openly kind while continuing to follow his dreams.

Today, Jim continues to be successful in his career. His family relationships are doing well. Even though it may be challenging for Jim due to his intense sensitivities and soft heart, he is now able to self-soothe and be clear about what works for him and what does not in a kind manner. Jim has improved his inner and outer boundaries. With a common language and understanding, Jim and his family as well as his associates have healthier relationships, and everyone reports better communication and relationships.

GRATITUDE

This is a topic rich in meaning and increasingly common in discussions. There are several facets of gratitude that add to the spiritual juice of life. To be grateful is different than having gratitude. There is a paradigm difference that intensely sensitive people can be impacted by in profound ways.

To have gratitude is a mental construct that implies possessing something that you can choose to keep or give away. You have gratitude typically regarding a person's actions, place, or event. It is an outside generated experience.

To be grateful is to "be" the thing you wish to humbly offer; allowing it to emerge through you. To be grateful is a flow or a way of being in the sense that the gratitude vibe is evident in all of you. You become the gratitude that emanates from your being. In real terms, you are the gratitude, you do not possess the gratitude.

To be grateful is a way of living that transcends events and personalities because it is an inner reality that you allow the world to experience through you. You are not giving or receiving gratitude, you are Gratitude in expression.

Being grateful is frequently noted in more than one area. Your inner gratitude when things are going well for you may have one type of feeling. Being grateful in the face of some sort of adversity is another hallmark of your real level of inner gratefulness. It is easy to look and feel grateful when things are going your way. Are you also expressing deep gratitude when faced with life's obstacles or challenges? Your answer to this question can help you differentiate between having gratitude and being grateful.

The third notable area is being grateful for gratitude's sake. This is where the mental construct has deepened through your emotions and now emanates from within your being. People comment on your way of seeing things. Your tolerance for adversarial and toxic situations diminishes. You choose the way of gratitude no matter what is happening around you.

As an intensely sensitive person who wants to live a juicy life, you become more and more aware of the impact of anything other than gratitude with others who are developing a deep sense of authentic inner gratitude. From the inside out, allow your intensely sensitive awareness to open to inner gratitude coming from within and move into your outer world. You will experience success and fulfillment on every level regardless of circumstance. The more flow, the sweeter the juice!

Meet Betty

Betty was a mentor and confidant to all the teenagers in her neighborhood. Her guidance was valuable to her own children and their friends. She had an uncanny way of relating to them that helped them through the many challenges of adolescence. Betty would deeply listen with a safe and supportive ear. She was often heard teaching them ways to deal with their parents so they could be heard. Betty was loved by so many people.

Interestingly, Betty was denied the closeness of a family as she grew up. The youngest of 5 with strong willed parents, Betty's sensitivities and intensity had to be stuffed and hidden so she wouldn't get into trouble. She would share how she had to hide any tears and pretend that she never felt pain as a young girl. She learned many coping skills for dealing with pain that eventually led her to drinking alcohol excessively. Betty would tell others that she was never fully understood as a child. She carried so much complicated grief and old pain from her younger years.

Betty turned her pain and being misunderstood as a young girl into the compassion and listening ear she offered the teens later in life. Betty's ability to listen and understand the struggles were not an accident as she also walked those similar roads.

I knew Betty. We would speak at times about her care and love for the youth. She would say that she was grateful for their liveli-hood, and she was happy to experience it with them! Betty was a kid at heart and finally, she was able to allow herself to be authentically grateful for her life and the lessons. Without the challenging times as a young girl, Betty would not have been as well equipped to help the teenagers later in her life. Now, years later, she looks back with grati-tude for the lessons.

When Betty passed away, her legacy was remembered by many people, now adults, that Betty helped through tough times. Betty is remembered fondly. It was her ability to be grateful in the face of her personal trials and obstacles that made Betty the amazing woman that she was to these young people in her life. Betty taught the young people to be grateful and her legacy lives on in the grateful hearts of those she touched so profoundly.

GIVING

You've heard it said that if you want something to come into your life, you must give it away first. Yes! How does this work and why is this part of a juicy, fulfilled life? Intensely sensitive people are nat-urally acutely aware of the flow in life. Giving and receiving are the same energetic flow and are necessary for ultimate satisfaction and fulfillment.

Yes, be a freely giving intensely sensitive person. Freely give of your time and talent while adhering to healthy, well-defined boundaries. Squishy boundaries or undefined boundaries cause confusion and ultimately wreak havoc in your life. You will know when you are out of alignment because you will be tired or weary, frustrated, or intolerant and maybe even short tempered. The idea is to be aware and pay attention.

The goal is to give freely within your pre-defined boundaries which allows the space and opportunity for you to receive from others and the world at large. Both giving and receiving are opposite sides of the same coin. As you share and give, you allow for the entry of great fulfillment to come into the space you created by the giving. Think of this as your breathing. Your exhale is the give. Your inhale is the receive. One without the other is not going to serve you or anyone else for that matter.

When you live by this higher principle of freely giving, freely receiving, your sensitivities can relax a bit and you will experience a smoother day to day life. By honoring this principle, you begin to give from your overflow. This ensures that you do not deplete yourself, even if you are tempted. Becoming depleted is an expense that only creates challenges and burnout. Stopping the flow, like stopping your breath, yields anxiety, angst and eventually some sort of eruption. Your flow comes from your overflow while you retain your inner energetic integrity. The old idea of giving without regard for your own well-being is outdated and does not serve you or anyone else.

Intensely sensitive people live best when their flow has inner alignment and is present in daily life. Give yourself some care, support, focus and kindness. Receive that and more as the universe conspires to fulfill your every want and need. The key: let go and give away what no longer serves you. Most people start giving away stuff. This is a good start. Remember that life happens from inside out so giving stuff first addresses the effect of the cause of inner "stuff". I suggest you begin to freely give away fears, doubts, worries, grief, and guilt. In your quiet time, allow these to go to another location in the universe where they will serve. Let them go – give them away. Then breathe in goodness and kindness and love, gratitude, and compassion. Do this daily until it becomes natural to let the others pass by like clouds and there is no longer a place for them any longer.

Keep the flow going. First give away what no longer serves you on all levels. Then, allow yourself to receive what is meant for you. Often this will not be as you expect or imagine. I suggest you give away expectations and begin to trust that your intensely sensitive life is meant to be much grander than you expect or can see in the moment. This is where Universal trust enters.

If you always give and refuse to receive knowingly or unknowingly, you will suffer resentment, weariness, and frustration. Receiving is not the same as taking. Receiving is part of the flow of the Universe. It starts with something as simple as a compliment. What else are you cheating yourself from that is trying to come into your life?

Many people I work with initially have a challenging time with receiving. I believe that many of us are culturally trained to deny our own needs and wants for the sake of others. This conditioning has made receiving a bit difficult or downright hard for so many people. Only exhaling and never inhaling is out of balance. Holding your breath causes anxiety in the system and keeps your biology on alert. Being out of rhythm in breath and giving/receiving both cause angst. If you are struggling with receiving for any reason, the time is now to examine this and make some inner changes. Remember, to receive is part of life and is very different from taking in motive and consciousness.

Meet Jean

Jean is a nurse. She is always giving at work and at home. In fact, Jean is the one all her friends call when they want any kind of advice because they know she will listen and help them no matter what is happening in Jean's life at that moment. She even shared with me that "I take on the energy of my patients as I work with them." She also had no way to discharge that energy, so she was carrying it around with her knowingly and unknowingly. Jean is a giving person. Jean has some personal struggles caused by over-giving coupled with an unconscious belief that she doesn't deserve to receive. Jean has a hard time receiving love and care from others. Her marriage was suffering and her relationship with other family members was strained because she often deflects and does not allow others to give to her. Jean has expressed that even emotional support is hard for her to receive.

As a result, Jean was burned out and stressed which was causing many physical health challenges. She was irritable and often curt. She came to me with deep sadness saying that she gives all the time, and no one cares or gives back to her. She wants desperately to be cared about and loved and she is missing it because she over gives to the point of depletion. Jean was unable to receive the love and support from others she desperately wanted.

These struggles led Jean to seeking out a therapist and a group meeting to help her with her relationships. She wanted things to be more equitable rather than so one-sided. After months of therapy, Jean was still struggling, and she reported feeling more dejected and had lost hope that she could be fulfilled like she helped others feel fulfilled. Jean shared that she felt alone in her sensitivities and her way of "doing the world".

Jean and I worked together for some time individually and at times in small groups and workshops. Jean was open-minded and she was verbal about her struggles. She wanted to have her life be happier and more effective. Jean worked on developing multiple peer groups and seeking new leisure activities that fulfilled her social needs. Eventually, Jean was able to give to her family freely after a long day at work and she could receive care and love from her husband and children. Inner boundaries, self-care and reorienting her priorities were all components of Jean's growth into a more equitable and satisfying life.

By slowing down a little and breathing, Jean was able to feel her emotions and temper her intellectual sensitivities that were creating much of the angst and deflection of others. Jean reported more relaxation and better family harmony. Being intensely sensitive, Jean was able to use her intensity and her spiritual sensitivities to navigate her work and family life in a more fulfilling manner without taking on the pain of others and bringing it home.

Jean now reports that she is happier and experiencing more flow rather than frustration and irritation. She gives at work and to her loved ones and now she can also better receive what is being offered to her. Jean receives freely at work and home with minimal deflection. She said to me recently: "Giving and Receiving really are different sides of the same coin!"

Jean continues to practice her boundaries, discernment, and use of the principles to guide her inner world. We continue to work together from time to time as Jean has new awareness or new inquiries. Jean shared that "Having a mentor like you who gets me makes my life so much better. I am trusting myself more and more. Thank you."

It is all about human connection, psychological safety and understanding that intensely sensitive people require more connection than many might believe. The more sensitive and intense you are, the more important understanding supportive people make all the difference.

COMPASSION

Compassion can be defined as positive thoughts and feelings that foster the rise of hope, courage, determination, and inner strength. In the Buddhist tradition, compassion is the wish for another being to be free from suffering. Compassion has many operational definitions as well as a myriad of expressions.

Compassion is the root of forgiveness. The first order of action regarding compassion is looking within yourself and freely offering compassion to yourself for all the blunders, follies, and mistakes of being human. Yes, life is a rich amazing journey. Intense sensitives tend to be overly self-critical or self-denying. Both are a result of being intensely sensitive in an insensitive world. Compassion for self, for the grand adventure of being human is the cornerstone for your peace of mind and fulfillment. Sometimes this can seem impossible or elusive, I promise self-compassion is attainable.

Compassion for others and their journeys is also important. This does not mean you compromise yourself or put yourself in harm's way. You can have compassion from a distance and not humanly enter the lion's den knowingly. Compassion is a way of being, it is not a thing you have that you get to give away so you can feel better about yourself. Compassion is a way – not an event as many are fooled into believing.

Being internally gentle is a hallmark sign of a compassionate person. Are you gentle with your inner self? This does not mean being weak or a doormat. You can be gentle with firm boundaries when you know who you are and the principles by which you are living.

Be sure to always live by your higher principles. When you stray, return as soon as possible. This is not about perfectionism; it is about living authentically from the inside out. Intense sensitives respond deeply to everyday, ordinary life. This is a great gift. Cherish the richness and depth of your being.

Compassion is a vital part of your survival as a human being. When selfishness begins to surface, compassion may appear to be taking a back seat. In these times of awareness, take a few breaths and focus on your self-compassion and allow this to extend to others. This will help ease the tension of the egoic selfishness that can undermine your serenity and harmony.

More on compassion and compassion fatigue in Chapter XII.

Meet Lewis

Lewis is one amazingly compassionate man. He is a healer in many ways. Looking into his eyes, you can see and feel compassion coming from him. Lewis is welcoming and he shares his knowledge and gifts with others. He was introduced to me by a mutual friend. I was told that he was the most compassionate man before I met him.

When I met Lewis, he gave me a hug and he then rested his hand on my shoulder and said: "Rest here in my home and enjoy". Soon after, his 2 children and amazing wife came out to greet me and my friend. Lewis disappeared for a short time. While he was absent, all of us relaxed, had some light food and water and we laughed together.

Lewis returned with a gift he had just created for me. He told me that he could see my healing talents and that I was to rest and drink up the beauty of nature all about and rest in the company of friends. He had such intense and compassionate eyes and an easy presence to be around. I had not shared that I was on a trip, taking a break from a very stressful time in my life, yet somehow Lewis had the awareness. Lewis' compassion touched me deeply and through his compassion we connected, and I felt renewed in a few short hours.

Lewis shared with me that he, too, had "many demons" to fight in his youth. He now was able to freely offer compassion while maintaining his sense of inner integrity and giving away too much too quickly. As in all of life, there are seasons of great change, Lewis shared as we walked and talked. Our connection changed my life forever.

Compassion is the foundation of the art of forgiveness. Lewis had mastered this art of forgiveness and he was able to live from the place of compassion within his soul. Because of his compassion, I was profoundly impacted that day. Lewis knows his gifts and intense sensitivities are valuable and he uses them for the welfare of those around him. This is an example of the profound power that comes forth as you clear away the blocks and you allow your profound intense sensitivities to be channeled toward the greater Good.

Intensely sensitive people, like you, experience the world differently than many others. This is a gift! Your Spiritual Juice is the vital force that tells you that you are alive. You are swimming in this juice – it is the energy and substance from which you create your world.

Create a practice of pondering ideas and inspiration each day. By protecting and dedicating time to connect with your own true essence, you fill your heart with Joy and the substance of compassion. Following are some points to ponder.

Living first by spiritual principles relieves the stress and suffering an intensely sensitive person can experience. You live on a different plane – your normal is different from other normal. You are wonderfully created and have all you need within you for your happiness and success.

Take a few breaths and ponder these questions. You may want to journal your ideas.

Points to Ponder:

1. What are your foundational principles?

2. How do you express kindness and compassion?

3. Are you more apt to give or receive initially?

4. In what ways do you maintain your flow?

5. Where can you make effective changes?

6. How do you demonstrate gratitude in your daily life?

7. How do my inner and outer boundaries support my life's vision?

CHAPTER II.

Being Intensely Sensitive in an Insensitive World

Usually, people who are sensitive need more time to understand the real world.

~~ Sudha Murty

You are sensitive, right? Have you ever been told to "suck it up"? You are intense, right? Have you ever been told to "tone it down" or that "you are too much?" This culture largely discounts feelings, emotions, and intense sensitivity so you may have an inner battle going on about how to be the authentic you when an important part of you is denied, marginalized, or even criticized by the society. Have you ever wished you had less sensitivity or intensity? I'll bet these are the times that you struggled to be heard, understood, or accepted by those around you.

Your intensities and sensitivities are truly your inherent assets. They are part of your soul's calling, meant to bring your vision into reality. They offer you the opportunity to live a richer, more vibrant life. As you locate and associate with other intense sensitives, you will begin to calibrate your personal "normal". Your "normal" cannot be compared to others' "normal" because there is a qualitative difference in experience and acuity of feelings and awareness. Everyone's "normal" is different and this neurodiversity is beautiful. It may feel off putting at first and there is often a right/wrong discussion that is not relevant. This is your invitation to look deeper and beyond what you may already understand to truly appreciate and embrace the amazing variety of human experience.

The world continuously bombards you with stimulus that can be overwhelming to an intense sensitive. As someone who is intensely sensitive, you must take care of your environment differently than your non-intense sensitive friends and family. If fluorescent light bothers you, remove them from your environment as much as possible. Take focused action to create an environment that supports your fulfilled life rather than one that you must keep tolerating, accommodating, and thus diminishing your life experience.

Many intense sensitives struggle with addiction of various types as they cope with feeling everything so deeply that it becomes overwhelming, and any numbing agent seems like good relief. Eventually, the ultimate betrayal happens when what seemed to help ease the inner overwhelm and pain becomes the master and you, the slave. The problem here is that you can become so numb and distracted that your fulfillment as a person becomes elusive. The addictive behavior continues to erode your life force and drain your energy and soon you are betraying your own values and beliefs. What started out helping turns on you and now is trying to take you down.

As you take a stand for living by spiritual principles and resting on this foundation, your intense sensitivities begin to work in your favor. Your discernment and clarity are enhanced. Your life is fulfilled. Protect your foundation by dedicating time each day to connecting to your heart's desire and calling. Simply be with the inner knowing and breathe. By allowing your inner promptings to come to the surface, you will see your next right actions clearly.

Being intense and sensitive has unique depth. You will always be unfolding and evolving as you go through life. Evolving or devolving are your choice, and you can change your mind any time. You will not do everything in this book perfectly and there is no panacea or simple map for life. Your exploration, curiosity and keen perception will be your valuable assets on your road. Yes, the world often misunderstands you or does not get you. Yes, your life can be tricky and challenging. And your life is also glorious and affords you the opportunity to experience your authentic essence. With all its twists and turns, life, your life, is valuable and you are needed in this world.

Meet Polly

Polly is a talented, intense, sensitive woman. She is an introvert, and she struggles with social anxiety that stems from social awkwardness as a younger woman. Polly owns a small business and has a vast knowledge of business and personal relations. Polly is intensely sensitive, and she is trying to make it in an insensitive world.

Polly is sensitive to bright lights and certain loud noises. She has trouble in crowds when the noise level reaches a certain elevation. She has intense moods and can be quiet and melancholy or bright and talkative. Polly sees and understands many things intuitively. She is respected by many of her colleagues and her business associates and clients. Polly is creative, talented, successful, sensitive, and intense. Polly also struggles with being lonely, sad, intense, misunderstood and judged. Polly's intense sensitivities are respected by others, yet they are not able to see beyond the surface to the depth of experience she feels every moment.

Polly is an intensely sensitive person trying to make it in an insensitive world. What many do not understand is that she pays a marked price for being intensely sensitive and at times recharging her batteries seems impossible because of the constant drain on her energy reserves. When the drain becomes too much, Polly reports feeling anxious and unable to rest or feel rested after sleep. She shares that she can feel "like I am on edge, even when trying to meditate."

Polly is an example of someone who has developed many of her natural gifted talents into her life's work. She tells me that she has always had struggles with her sensitivities and has largely been misunderstood for most of her life. Polly shares that her heart wants to keep being present for others to support their intensities.

We talk often and we share our intensities with one another. We honor our multiple peer groups and the fact that today we are understood more often. Being intensely sensitive in an insensitive world is challenging. I think there are more of us intensely sensitives than I initially thought.

Being intensely sensitive in an insensitive world can be difficult and it can also be glorious. Being misunderstood or not believed can harm your self-esteem. You are fully equipped to fulfill your personal and unique life vision and mission. You do not need anyone's permission except your own. Being intensely sensitive brings great emotions and life experience. Remind yourself of your unique gifts and look within to begin to create inner safety.

Intuition

Intuition is the highest form of intelligence. Intuition comes in many forms. Your intuition is a vital part of your fuel. Your inner fuel tank is essential for your functioning. There are 4 major categories of intuition that overarch your experience. You may have more than 1 and just like intensities, they have different intensities, and they show up differently in everyone.

Here are the broad categories. Identify what you most resonate with today.

Clairsentience shows up as a feeling or a hunch. Following your gut or being able to discern the energy of others would be most applicable in this area.

Clairvoyance messages come as a scene, impression, or a metaphor. Most people would call this "psychic."

Clairaudience shows up as if someone is speaking to you in your mind's ears. You "hear" the messages and are prompted to pay attention. This is not a hallucination. Typically, they are short, concise messages and possibly not in the way you imagine.

Claircognizance is when your intellect gets what I call a "download" or the information becomes clear to you based on the information coming in through your intuitive channels.

Your intuition is a gift. Everyone has the gift. It shows up differently in different people. When you squash the gift, it eventually emerges. Most of the people I work with can identify their intuitive capacity on some levels yet have not fully embraced this important part of their unique intense sensitivities. Now is the time to release your apprehension about using your natural intuitive gifts. Getting more in touch with your intuition will serve you greatly moving forward.

How does your intuition and spiritual sensitivity show up for you? When was the last time you honored this part of you? How does your spiritual sensitivity play with your gifted intensities? How do you use them to be a beneficial presence? Trust your inner guidance more each day and you will be amazed at the results.

I teach people to verify and confirm as they learn to trust their inner guidance. The more you document and practice the more competence and confidence you will amass. Practice tuning in and trusting. This is a great journey. No, there is nothing wrong with you; in fact, there is something right with you that will be of great benefit as you explore your inner gifts.

Empathy

Empathy is the ability to feel and understand what is happening for another on a deep and meaningful level. Many empaths feel what is happening in another and around them in tangible ways. Add this to your overexcitabilities/intensities and this can be a powerful and profound combination. Learning how to navigate these in a meaningful way is important.

When your empathy is strong, your self-care and attention to your reality is vital for your success. Many people may take this energy expenditure for granted yet it is vital that you replenish your inner resources regularly. As with your intuition, these sensitivities require inner fuel and resources to be their best. Self-care, self-awareness, and self-compassion are essential for your growth and health.

Your empathy may come through in varied ways. You may be able to truly connect to another's perspective or feel within your body what they are feeling. These experiences are very real and valid. Again, when you combine your intuition, and your intensities with your empathic ability there is a great triangle for strength and personal power. You may experience challenges and have some difficulty with this intense trio. It is vital that you access support from peers and guides to help validate your experience and show you ways to navigate a world that does not encourage or support this deep way of being.

Boundaries and knowing what is for you to do and not do is essential to retaining your inner resources and not becoming burned out or experiencing compassion fatigue. Your inner boundaries are very important. I share with my clients that their sense of self means knowing what they have to offer and not offering it too quickly. It is tempting to give too much too fast and create a crisis. This is not the goal.

Meet Julie

Julie is a scientist, and she loves her job. Julie says that her several decade career has afforded her many great opportunities. She has a great mind for statistics, research, and synthesizing research results. In fact, many of her esteemed colleagues are sometimes confounded by her ability to see results and trends that are accurate yet not obvious. Julie uses her intuition as a valuable resource. She shared that because she is one of a few women, that the men tend to initially marginalize her input until their results confirm her findings. Using her intuition is natural for Julie and she did not even realize that is what she was using until we started talking about intuition and she had that Ah-Ha moment!

Julie also has strong empathy that has caused her many interpersonal challenges over the years. She has had a hard time distinguishing what is hers and what is another's' emotion, so she has been taking on all emotions of everyone around her. Needless to say, Julie became tired and burned out. She was wondering if she was depressed and needed medication. Julie heard one of my *Someone Gets Me* podcast episodes and she called.

What our discussion has revealed is that Julie is a multipotentialitie and she has an intensely sensitive nature coupled with precise intellectual ability. Julie's talents are perfect for her chosen vocation, yet they are not often appreciated by colleagues. I believe this is because the colleagues are not sure how to engage with someone who is creative, intuitive, empathic, and cognitively intelligent. Her intensities are part of her everyday life. As Julie has learned more and made friends with her overexcitabilities, she has gained confidence and competence in using her gifted intensities.

Empathy and discernment in relationships of all kinds is a bit more challenging at times. Julie cares so deeply and can often see solutions that others cannot because of her intuition (sensitivities) and intensities that she becomes frustrated. This is where there are many opportunities for self-exploration and redefining inner boundaries. The more aware Julie becomes, the more effective her boundaries, the happier and satisfied she becomes.

What do Julie's adult children have to say? They have reported being happy to see their mom less stressed and having more fun. She has moved through much of the pain from old grief and is now enjoying her family in a whole new way. Julie's empathy helps her in her work and family life, and she now can set healthy inner boundaries to maintain her sovereignty and personal integrity.

As Julie and I have shared many times, the more we understand and the more we make friends with our unique intensities and sensitivities, the more amazing and beautiful life becomes. It is worth the work to dive into the messiness because the pay-off is remarkable. Ponder these questions. Be willing to delve into your inner world. Your authentic self is truly amazing!

Points to Ponder:

1. How do your intense sensitivities show up in your life?

2. How do you handle the insensitivity of the world at large?

3. In what ways have you adjusted to survive in an insensitive world?

4. What can you improve to make your life even more vibrant and satisfying?

5. What overexcitabilities are you managing effectively in daily life?

6. What sensitivities are you using in your favor?

CHAPTER III.

Creating Personal Safety

Safety starts with knowing that your intuition about people is a brilliant guardian.

~~ *Gavin de Becker*

Personal safety is vitally important. I am speaking of safety on many levels. Intense sensitives often feel a sort of fear or trepidation that underlies events and experiences. This existential fear can look like social anxiety, overwork, disconnection and numbing behaviors. Establishing and maintaining personal safety within and without is necessary for your mental and physical well-being.

Safety emotionally may require that you educate others about your intensities and then teach them ways to effectively relate with you. You may also want to learn and understand your personal limits and be willing to act on them by creating and maintaining a safe space for your expression. We will talk about boundaries later in this book. Boundaries are necessary for you to maintain.

Physical safety is also important. Intense sensitives often feel warnings before others. Learn to discern a viable warning coming through your sensitivities and a fear/anxiety response. As an intense sensitive, you will handle both differently.

As you honor your personal and unique intense sensitivities, you will know where your healthy, functional boundaries lie. To create a personal safety plan is effective in dealing with loud vexations and other challenges for intense sensitives.

Here are some action steps:

1. Identify your safe zone within mentally, emotionally, physically, spiritually, and socially life areas.

2. Make friends with yourself, your inner gifts, and sensitivities.

3. Identify your personal thresholds and be willing to make changes that honor you.

4. Act in ways that support your intense sensitivity.

5. Maintain supportive human connections to share life's ups and downs.

Psychological Safety

For intensely sensitive people, psychological safety is a necessity to help reduce anxiety and overwhelm. You can feel the overarching energy of a group or event and it impacts your inner sense of safety without a word being spoken. Psychological safety is the shared belief that it's safe to take interpersonal risks within your peer group or family. These risks include speaking up when you have a need or are having a problem, being heard when you speak without ridicule and off-color humor, you feel safe engaging and sharing ideas, and you and others are open to self-development and increased self-awareness. In other words, you are safe to be you without the fear of retribution.

You know you are psychologically safe when you can share your ideas without fear of ridicule even if you are challenging the status quo or existing way of operating. Without the safety to learn and grow and ask discerning questions, intensely sensitive people often shut down which can adversely impact their work and relationships.

All too often, work environments and families can lack psychological safety due to fears, grief, trauma or simply not being aware or paying attention. Intensely sensitive people are aware of the safety issue even when there are no words.

Psychological safety is identified as open, honest communication that has authenticity and care for all participants. Clear, consistent rules of engagement are identifiable by all individuals. As yourself, "Do I feel supported and valued in this environment?" Pay attention to your inner voice as well as external clues. Be honest.

Be willing to stand in your sovereignty while also being open to learning and growing. As you release old beliefs and patterns, your sense of safety will adjust. Pay attention and honor your experience.

The *Someone Gets Me* podcast has an episode on Psychological Safety in the workplace. This may be of interest for your professional life.

Meet Sally

Sally is a fast-thinking and fast-moving woman. She recently divorced her husband and is now embarking on the next phase of her life. The divorce is not salient to the story, yet Sally does state that her fast-thinking brain and her unending energy were challenges at times in her marriage as well as her family life as a young girl.

Sally can move so fast that it feels like the Tasmanian Devil, a whirling dervish type of feel. She can exhaust others by her fast speech and physical excitabilities. Sally is either on or off and she is mostly on. She has many divergent interests, and she is a very creative visionary. Sally is also a neuroscientist and college professor.

Sally moves so fast in her sensitivities that she often misses the social cues within her relationships in work and school. Sally came to me seeking assistance with negotiating some unpleasant school relationships and interactions. Sally was struggling and was having flashbacks and anxiety that she could relate to her childhood and being misunderstood. Sadly, she was again experiencing judgment focused on her intelligence and drive to do well. Sally shared that her performance in the classroom and faculty meetings seemed to be declining. She stated that she was experiencing impostor syndrome and wanted to have her performance be aligned with her skills and expertise in a productive and successful way.

We explored her drive and focus regarding her and her students' success and accomplishments. She realized that underneath this intense drive was a secret fear of not being enough, impostor syndrome.

So, overcompensating and being the best blanketed the pain of not belonging and fear of not being enough. This woman uncovered an internalized belief that was causing her to overuse her sensitivities which then created some additional emotional pain. In a real sense, school became an emotionally unsafe place until Sally was able to work through the miscues and choose differently. As she was able to see that the challenges were generated through the window of her beliefs, Sally became empowered to heal and rectify what was not serving her which allowed her the opportunity to step fully into her own competence with confidence.

With practice and support, Sally is now using her intense sensitivities to further her career and her vision for her life. She struggles less with being misunderstood. Sally told me recently that she is happy to have her intensity and her sensitivities even though she has a hard time with new people at first. Sally is now using her skills with more poise. Her insight into ways to authentically present herself are easing her struggles. Safety is paramount as we will only grow to the level of safety we feel. Sally is creating safety for herself, and she is open to her new opportunities. Sally also has learned better boundaries with others, so she is able to remain in integrity. As for Sally's co-faculty and students, they are inspired by her awareness. She is now mentoring others.

Points to Ponder:

1. What does safety mean to you?

2. How is psychological safety present in your work and home environments?

3. Safety and thriving go hand in hand. Ponder how they interact in your life. Are there any adjustments you wish to make?

CHAPTER IV.

Making Friends with Your Intense Sensitivities

The privilege of a lifetime is being who you are.

~~ *Joseph Campbell*

Making friends with yourself is sometimes challenging. Are you one of those individuals who is hard on yourself, maybe even judgmental or overly critical? Are you able to forgive yourself as easily as you forgive others? Many intensely sensitive people treat themselves mercilessly, often judging themselves harshly. What you may think are liabilities may actually be your allies and assets when you make friends with those parts of you!

It is important that you take the time to befriend yourself. Making friends with you and your intense sensitivities helps you acknowledge and appreciate who you are from the inside out. We all get frustrated with ourselves at times. It is important to not weaponize your frustration and turn it into a bat to beat yourself up with each day. Being intense and sensitive has many challenging experiences that you may experience. Be sure to focus on being a great friend to all the versions of you.

If you are not friendly in your thoughts, words, and actions toward you then you will experience increased life turbulence and possible loneliness. Your intensities and sensitivities are a gift, even when they don't feel like a gift. Sometimes you may experience them as a double-edged sword. Intensities can feel like a flood of emotion or thoughts that are never ending at some points and also be like a void or a sense of nothingness at other times. This range of experience can be exhausting when we do not have a deep understanding and relationship with our inner nature.

I imagine many of your life challenges are being blamed on your intensity or sensitivity or both. If only I wasn't so sensitive. Why are you so intense? Can't you calm down and stop? Why do you think so much? All these and more are things that you may have heard or may say to yourself. Recently, someone said to me, "Do you have to think so much and feel so much? Can't you just coast like everyone else?"

The list goes on as we live life and engage with people who do not experience deep intensities and sensitivities. This is a great awareness that helps us release judgment or criticism of self or others. The diversity is beautiful, not something to discount in any way.

It is time to share some compassion toward you. Compassion for the great adventure of being alive. Self-blame and self-deprecation do not motivate, they erode your life in insidious ways. Whether you can see it now or not, you are uniquely talented and gifted with the perfect combination of intense sensitivities to fulfill your life's vision. Your journey includes releasing old, outdated beliefs and seeing your intensities and sensitivities from a fresh and amazing perspective.

If you were made fun of or even chastised for your intense sensitivities, it is time to gain perspective. Just because someone, anyone, judges or assesses your intensities doesn't mean they are correct. It means they are judging themselves and projecting it on you, so they don't have to look at themselves consciously or unconsciously.

On behalf of the society at large, accept my sincere apology for the pain and betrayal that you have suffered because of ignorance. They know not what they are doing.

When I was younger, I showed my emotionally intense sensitivities. I would laugh hard, and I cried when I could feel others' pain. Over time I received messages from others that this intense emotional sensitivity was bad or wrong somehow. Even my mother, who was an empath, used to say: "Your bladder is too close to your eyes". My other family members also accused me of faking or making up my feelings, yet they were very real and very intense. This was a very lonely time for me. No one seemed to understand me.

In my teens and early twenties, I shut down and withdrew as I believed the people of my youth, that I was flawed and that my emotional intensities were bad or that I was making it all up. I was beginning to connect with my spiritual intensities during this time. I shared some of my intuitive ideas and was made fun of by others. I knew it was real yet the others in my life did not believe me.

Fast forward many years. It is my emotional and spiritual intense sensitivity that is the conduit for my unique ability to connect deeply with my clients and audience. What I was told in my youth was a liability is now an asset. Now that I understand and can use my intensity for the good rather than pushing it down in denial or fear and ultimately having a tolerance break, I am able to feel happy and live my heart's vision. A tolerance break is when the pain and disconnection come out in intense and messy ways. I could no longer deny my intensities and who I was as an intense, sensitive, powerful woman. Trying to pretend I was something different was unbearable.

Making friends with my inner intense sensitivities has brought great joy and compassion. I use this gift to fulfill my life's vision and to help others in living their most authentic life. In living our most authentic life, we experience hope emerging from within that is the fuel for our soul's calling. To see more resources and to connect further, visit www.visionsapplied.com.

Part of making friends with your intense sensitivities is beginning to nurture and care for you on deeper levels. Your life experiences and the way to engage with the world around you is experientially different than others who are not intensely sensitive. Maybe as a young person, you struggled to be understood. Maybe you have gifted and intense children who crave and need understanding and compassion.

Nurturing your intellect and emotions is as important as nurturing your physical and spiritual self. Developing your personal connection to the world around you is the glue that keeps you grounded and allows you to soar. In the event others do not understand you, keep looking. You will develop multiple peer groups over time. Each group serves one or several of your unique facets.

There are five forms of overexcitability as described by Dabrowski. They are sensual, psychomotor, intellectual, emotional, and imaginational. I prefer to refer to these qualities as intensities because many of my clients have misunderstood the word overexcitability and erroneously labeled it a liability or problem to be solved. I do not believe this was Dabrowski's intent when he coined the term. There is more about this coming up!

Teachers, parents, and others who are not aware of these gifts can misinterpret and label these gifts as problems. The truth is, some of the expressions of overexcitabilities, if allowed to run without focus and direction, can cause challenges for the individual and those around them. Some intensities may mimic other challenges like anxiety, depression, and ADHD for example.

I have worked with many clients over the years who have had difficult life challenges resulting from misunderstanding their own world of being intensely sensitive. Part of your inner work is in making friends with and honoring your specific intensities and sensitivities. When you have intensity of experience coupled with spiritual sensitivity, there are special needs that you may have to help you navigate this often-insensitive world. This does not mean there is something wrong with you, rather it means that you have a beautiful and unique make-up that, when honored, is amazing.

Sensitivities Explained

All people have a level of sensitivity. Many of us have multiple sensitivities. For me, and the purposes of this book, sensitivities include your spiritual connection and ability to feel and experience energy. Sensitivities can come in the form of deep empathy, clairvoyance, clairaudience, and a deep sense of knowing what is not immediately intellectually available.

Many people with intensities or overexcitabilities also have a sensitivity to the ethereal. Many have a keen intuitive ability that enhances their gifts. This synergy of inherent gifts can feel awkward, awe inspiring, "normal", or even mysterious. What matters most is embracing your unique experience with your sensitivities and intensities. Your intense sensitivities are unique to you for the fulfillment of your personal vision. You arrived with a vision and hope. Now is the time to bring them forth with focus.

Overexcitabilities or Intensities Explained

Let's look at the overexcitabilities as described by Kazimierz Dąbrowski, a Polish psychologist, psychiatrist, and physician. They can mimic diagnosis and they show up differently in different people. I will attempt to give you a flavor of what it is like to live with each intensity. Keep in mind that the ways things show up are as varied as the people who have the intensity. Some people have varying degrees of intensity and can have more than one.

As you are probably seeing here, each bright, gifted and intensely sensitive person possesses unique qualities that set them apart in some way from others. Thus, a peer group of those who understand as well as psychological safety at home, school/work are paramount for your success. There can be great achievement and great success. This is one of the many reasons why my intuitive mentoring work with intensely sensitive people is so rewarding and amazing.

Each overexcitability or intensity has different ways of showing up in daily life. Let's explore some of the ways you can identify these intensities in you or a loved one. For more information beyond the function of this book, I invite you to research Dabrowski further. For the purposes of this text, a functional understanding is most vital.

Sensual Overexcitability or Intensity

Sensual overexcitability is all about your senses. You most likely see acutely, taste with precision and can smell undertones in subtle ways. This heightened sensory awareness can make fluorescent lights or other electronics difficult as you may not be able to focus or relax. One of my clients has an intensity of smell. She uses it to create amazing perfumes and fragrance oil blends. Another client is a chef, and he uses his intensity to create food and sauces that are outstanding. With focus and following their inner vision, these two can use their sensual intensity to serve themselves and others. You may even express how you are feeling using your senses which may need some support or interpretation. For me, tags in clothes are particularly challenging and I have a tennis player client who is very sensitive to the seams in his socks! These are sensual intensities in daily life. Self-soothing is a necessary skill for all of us with a sensual overexcitability. The intensity can be calmed by finding a healthy outlet like petting a cat or dog, a healthy hug, a weighted blanket, or a relaxing bath.

Psychomotor Overexcitability or Intensity

Psychomotor overexcitability is positively correlated with many gifted traits. The folks I know with this overexcitability are moving nearly all the time. They usually love exercise or sports of some kind. They bring their mental focus and intellect to their moving, so they tend to excel. Sometimes people call themselves too active or hyper. I tend to focus on healthy ways to channel the intensity and be active, pursue sports that are of interest and allow your intellect to come along as you achieve success with your competitive focus. You need to be able to express your physical intensity. Find avenues of expression so you do not create anxiety or unfulfilled dreams by holding yourself back. Great tennis players could be seen in this area as tennis is like a moving chess match. Learn meditation and other relaxing techniques to give your body rest. Many of my clients seek nature as the catalyst to give their body and mind the much-needed relaxation so they can recharge in a healthy manner.

Intellectual Overexcitability or Intensity

Intellectual overexcitability manifests most often as being unbelievably curious and incessantly asking questions. You may have a voracious appetite for learning and knowledge or even intellectual debating or competition. Because our culture is so intellectually driven, this intensity can get over rewarded and you may have the idea that this is all there is to being gifted, intense or sensitive. When you are not mentally stimulated, you may daydream or lose focus. This is a message to put yourself in a place where you can be challenged, and you can follow your questions until you are satisfied. The stressors here show up in what I call "Playing dead on the highway syndrome." This means projecting your overthinking into the future and thinking of all the things that can go wrong to the exclusion of what can go right. Thus, you create anxiety and stress by using your intellectual intensity with focus that is not serving you. If this is you, then learning ways to channel your intellect and ask better questions can help ease your mind.

Emotional Overexcitability or Intensity

Emotional overexcitability is most likely the most common with my clients. High emotions and intensity of feeling experience categories most of my clients over the years. If your emotions are intense and can even seem extreme or very complex, then you may have this intensity. Your great and positive emotions are experienced as awesome and powerful while your negative emotions can be so intense that you feel disempowered or even crippled until the storm passes. If your emotions are deep and intense and you struggle at times to verbally express what you are feeling because words are pedestrian in these matters, then you may want to make friends with your emotional overexcitability.

I have a teenager that I work with who experiences depth of her emotional experience and she has always thought something was wrong with her because her sister doesn't experience feelings the same way. Their parents went to so many doctors and psychologists, looking for a diagnosis yet there was nothing wrong clinically. This young girl is working with an emotional overexcitability. Over time she is learning to calm her storms and use some of her intensity as part of her creative pursuits. She is also learning that many of her somatic complaints are emotionally based. There are different strategies for helping her with emotional intensities rather than constant medical tests that keep yielding no medical problems. It is also important for her to realize she is not making it up and that the somatic issues are real, AND they are coming from an overexcitability, not a disease or illness.

Her parents are learning how to support her and show her the way to focus her intense sensitivities. Come to find out, her mother also has this intensity and has lived her entire life thinking she was some sort of anomaly when in fact she is not. Now, everyone in the family has a whole new paradigm and view of emotional health and intensities with which to work within. This is one of the families that I use the word intensity more frequently, so they do not take on a negative label. The goal is the empowered use of intense sensitivities in daily life.

Imaginational Overexcitability or Intensity

Imaginational overexcitability is all about your imagination and your fantastic life. When you have the intensity, you can see solutions and vision beyond what seems possible. Your fantasy life is rich and vibrant. You could develop amazing games, movies, or novels. Many would stand in awe of your creativity and imagination yet to you it seems normal. You might even wonder what the big deal is that others are seeing in your ability until you begin to see that your imaginational overexcitability is actually real. I had a friend who came to my house one night and we were talking about overexcitabilities, and she finally understood and said: "So, it is a thing, really!" When she realized she had this overexcitability which makes her a great teacher, she relaxed and stopped trying to fix what she thought was wrong with herself. She is now excelling with her "imaginations" in her business.

Sometimes it is your simple awareness and validation along with some information that is all you need to make better friends with yourself and your gifts.

With awareness and understanding comes the ability to make supportive and helpful decisions for you and those around you. I find that everyone is freer and calmer as they learn about these intensities and how to work with them. After the relief of awareness comes real focused action and work to have your intensities serve you rather than hinder you. It is not always easy, and I can share stories of people who declined to work with their intensities and create more pain for themselves. This is not my wish for you.

This book is meant to support you in the difficult and dark days as well as in the bright and empowering days. Sometimes the night can seem dark and distant. It is always helpful to have some valid understanding and support in your corner. A safety net if you will. The research, support, and understanding are being renewed and developed every day. Things are changing in our understanding as a gifted community. It is vital to learn as much as you can and apply the great wisdom that is available. You are not alone, even when it seems so.

What are Intense Sensitivities?

The term *intense sensitivities* is the way I describe someone with one or more overexcitability or intensity coupled with spiritual sensitivity in the form of intuition, deep knowingness, empathy, and the like. Many people who have intensities also share some unique spiritual gifts that may go undisclosed or even be taken for granted.

In my professional experience, there is a qualitative difference in the function and experience of the intensity when the person also has spiritual sensitivities. Knowing things before they happen or "seeing" what others cannot or do not see can be disconcerting. Learning how to use your intense sensitivities to fulfill your life's vision can be thrilling and challenging as you explore the depth of your unique gifts.

Intense sensitivities are not emotionally out of control behaviors or temper tantrums. This term describes a coming together of your natural spiritual gifts along with your overexcitabilities as a gifted person. In this combination, there is magic, awe, and profound life richness.

By understanding the interaction and synergy of both intensities and sensitivities, you have a unique perspective on this powerful and often confusing life experience. For many of the intensely sensitive people I have worked with, they feel everything or nothing at all due to the intensity of their sensitive systems.

There is a qualitative variance that points to an even more vivid and deep experience. I notice a lot of substance abuse challenges used to cope with that can feel insurmountable energy running through the brain and body. Some intensely sensitive people have keen intuition that can be uncomfortable and disconcerting.

Being highly intuitive and sensitive to energy in others as well as places can be signs of intense sensitivities. Spiritual Connection is a hallmark of this combination. Different from religion, spiritual connection is an intimate connection to the flow and essence of nature and cosmos. The elegant simplicity of the Universe is experienced in deeply moving ways.

Your intense sensitivities are a perfect and unique combination of intensities, sensitivities with varied amounts of each. You are here fully equipped to do what ought to be done by you. By trusting your unique gifted make-up, you are able to live your dream.

Meet Rachel

Rachel is a high energy, fast thinking, emotionally sensitive and unique character. She comes from a conservative family that is gifted and intensely sensitive. For Rachel and her family, this high level of functioning and fast paced life is the norm. In fact, Rachel and her family had no idea there was the term gifted. When I presented this information to assist Rachel become more aware of her intensities and how to use them for her benefit, she resonated and sat back, breathed a big sigh of relief, and said, "So this is what it is called." She was referring to her never ending energy and visionary ideas and propensity to see how to make money with ease.

Some of her family also could see the application of the information yet they denied that there was anything to consider as far as learning, focus, or success. The others simply reported that, "We just push through with our willpower, and we prevail. When we don't, we approach with more energy again." This presented a quandary for Rachel, as she was more aware of the challenges and more open and receptive to learning new and effective ways to approach her life and goals.

Rachel also had some denial about how she was being perceived by others because she was moving so fast. She reported trouble in school growing up and trouble in her adult relationships. She had insulated herself professionally by choosing largely solitary work environments. Rachel expressed deep sadness due to not fitting in since she was young and feeling alone, even within her family. She would become tearful and vulnerable then quickly keep talking as if to distract or medicate her feelings with incessant words. Stopping to breathe was difficult for Rachel initially.

We worked together several times a week initially to focus on making friends with herself rather than being so hard and critical. She excels and can see great solutions, yet she was unmerciful in her self-talk. Rachel reluctantly began to spend time each day in silence, looking within. At first, she did not report any improvement even though she was doing the work. I explained that breaking a generational and lifetime pattern takes some time and focus as well as perseverance. Rachel was tenacious and she stayed steadfast and worked on becoming quieter internally. She found that spending time on the beach or near the water was helpful.

Over time, Rachel began to identify and make friends with her own inner light and inner guidance. She became familiar with accessing her inner wisdom. Her discernment began to become more reliable because she was less distracted. Rachel was growing and transforming in many ways. Her husband did not like these changes. He often ridiculed and attempted to control her actions. We all met in person, and he was able to hear me yet declined to be open to any ideas other than his own. He was accustomed to the way things were and he did not see any need for humoring her want for change because he did not believe she would stick with this choice. He became more upset the more she changed. He simply did not think it would stick. I explained to him and Rachel that a family is like a mobile, when one of the people moves, it impacts and moves the entire system. When everyone is connected, the change in one person necessarily affects all the other people. He agreed in theory yet continued to struggle with her "bull-headed" decisions.

They were and are committed to the marriage and family so both kept focused on creating a way to make things work for everyone, including the children who are also gifted, sensitive, and intense.

As Rachel learned how to work with her intensities and use them to serve a higher good, she became more alive and the depression and anxiety she complained of initially was gone. She attributed her being clear on her vision and her goals as the impetus to increased self-love and connection.

Fast forward, Rachel has made some career changes that more align with her vocation and calling. She and her husband are happier. The children are once again excelling in school and extracurricular activities. The family is honoring everyone's differences and similarities with more compassion and understanding. When there are challenges and intense times, we talk about them and see the most profitable action for all concerned. Being the gifted mentor for Rachel and her family is a great honor and joy. They are working through blind spots and building effective family systems. The story continues and I am sure that with the ups and downs of life, Rachel and her family will continue to make friends with their giftedness, sensitivities, and intensities.

Spiritual Giftedness

Many gifted people have an uncanny sense of what is going on around them in atypical ways. This sensitivity to the spiritual or astral planes is available in varying ways to everyone, yet gifted people often have a unique connection and awareness. This spiritual intelligence is nuanced and you will most likely experience your connection in a very personal and unique manner.

Do you use your spiritual resources to solve problems? Is your reverence for all life so palpable that it transcends the material and physical world? Have you struggled with over giving because of empathy or kindness to others. Do you see the Spiritual in everyday living? If you are saying "yes" or even "maybe" to some of these, then your spiritual connection is alive and well.

Many do not use the word intuition or psychic because of the bad rap these words can have in certain areas. This is particularly true if the individual has been overly reinforced for intellectual ability to the exclusion of spiritual and emotional sensitivities. You may have experienced moments of boundless connection and Joy or even receiving information ahead of linear time. Intensely sensitive people often have a sense of what is about to transpire on some level. This includes picking up your phone and it starts ringing because the person you are thinking about is calling. It can also include having a "sense" of danger and taking another road home from work only to find out there was an accident on your typical path.

Spiritual giftedness can appear in many ways. It can be a longing for that something greater or a sense of deeper meaning to life. It also shows up in wanting your heart's desire to shine into the world. Some say there is a compelling feeling within to make a difference in some way. Spiritual connection is a sense of closeness to nature and elegant simplicity of the Universe as we know it today and beyond.

I also notice that many men have shut down their spiritual giftedness or may be in denial that they have these skills. Yet, Einstein noted that much of his genius was not linear or intellectual alone. There are many people who speak of their intuition as a vital aspect of their craft. Each person is speaking about spiritual giftedness in all its varied expressions.

"Sometimes I just know things" said one of my clients while another reported having goose bumps when certain information was popping into his head. My personal experience with spiritual giftedness is that many of the people that I have helped with addiction issues have unique spiritual sensitivities that were either being ignored or shut down intentionally.

The healing is in rectifying this inner schism. Addiction in all its forms comes from trying to fill an unfillable hole - using physical means to solve a spiritual problem. By coming into harmony with your inner spiritual sensitivities and owning how these sensitivities play with your intensities is the magic sauce that invites out all your subtle and not so subtle nuances and gifts.

Many of the gang leaders in prison are gifted and intensely sensitive as are others who have used the gift wrongly while some got stuck in the avoidance and self-deprecating dance, allowing that deep shame to drive maladaptive behaviors. Underneath all the trauma and problems is a person with a gifted, sensitive, intense soul trying to make it in the world. This does not in any way excuse errant behavior. I do believe that with understanding the door is opened to the possibility of rehabilitation, restoration, and recovery.

We are all born with a level of purity of our soul. As life happens, the crystal-clear inner essence can become murky or muddied. Our responsibility as we grow is to clean the vessel. Typically, this begins around age 28-32 years old unless there are opportunities earlier in life to begin the process of reclaiming those parts that are stuck in the muddied parts of life.

Spiritual giftedness is an amazing aspect that is often overlooked in our linear and over intellectualized society. Many scientists that I know will admit that they use their intuition regularly and must find a way to present things in a scientific manner so they will be accepted, and their findings believed. It is not ok to say "I know" as an expression of spiritual knowledge. Somehow this is not trusted in our world, yet I find it refreshing.

Discernment, verification, confirmation, and responsibility are all vital aspects of spiritual giftedness in everyday life. Let us examine these.

Discernment

Discernment is using your perception in the absence of judgment to obtain spiritual guidance and understanding. This is quite different from judging though many people confuse the two. Judgment, simply said, assigns value while discernment is focused on perception and understanding.

Life is fluid and ever moving and expanding. With this understanding, you have the freedom and right to change your mind. This is the power of discernment. For example, you may be invited to an event, and you discern that it is not your style, i.e.: loud and crowded. It is perfectly alright to decline as on your impression without judging the event as wrong or bad. It simply is not for you in that moment. Later you may be speaking with a friend who ensures you that there will be outside spaces and that you can leave whenever you want to leave and they would love you to attend with them. You can change your mind and attend if you discern that it may work for you while giving yourself permission to leave if the noise or crowds become too much.

The key distinction between discernment and judgment is the assignment of value. When you say something is good or bad, that is a judgment. Discernment is paying attention within and aligning you thoughts, words, and actions in the moment without judgment of the event or people involved.

As you get to know your unique spiritual sensitivities, you will be able to discern the guidance you are receiving. Your understanding improves and you are free of judging. It is perfectly ok to be quiet and hold your impressions close to your heart.

Meet Grace

Grace is a twice exceptional adult with Spiritual giftedness and sensitivities. She reports her awareness of her spiritual giftedness coming to light during a difficult time in her life several years ago. She is a corporate professional woman. This confused her because her "intuitions" and "inner promptings" did not follow what she knew in the more corporate area of life.

When Grace and I met, she was verbal about her intuitive ideas and promptings. She would become afraid and then talk about her fears as if they were the intuitive promptings. Grace could not yet discern the intuitive information from her fear. Her internal process was so fast that she experienced it as one continuous flow. We worked on slowing down her inner intellectual dialogue and gaining connection to spiritual principled living.

Being spiritually gifted requires discernment and paying attention on multiple levels. Not all intuitive information comes clearly and sometimes it comes in pieces over time. I had Grace journal and track how fear interfered with her intuition. Currently, she is much more clear about how the different impressions appear and how to process and integrate her intellect and her intuition.

Learning to verify and confirm the insight and intuitions that Grace received has helped with her discernment and has helped build her confidence.

Verification

Verification is the process of establishing the truth, accuracy, or validity of the intuitive message. I always say to verify the information. Asking does this feel right? How do I know I am accurate and what is my confidence rating for the information I am perceiving?

When you are tired, your accuracy often goes down so verifying your intuitive information is a vital part of developing confidence and competence in using intuition as part of your life.

I suggest keeping a journal where you document your intuitive insights. You will then be able to have accurate documentation on your insights to verify. Memory changes over time so thinking you will remember is not reliable for verification purposes.

Confirmation

Confirmation is ensuring the truth, strengthening, or substantiating the message. Very similar to verification, confirmation substantiates your findings and impressions. Sometimes Confirmation may take some time to determine. Still, confirming as much as you can is vital. This will help you see trends and avenues your spiritual intelligence speaks to you. Remember that spiritual timing is independent of human time.

I have had impression that I journaled be revealed 2 years after the journaling message. I knew it when I saw it happening and as I went back into my journal, I found the writing and was in awe as to the accuracy. In the days of immediate gratification, you may be tempted to be distracted. Pay attention and learn to trust your inner voice, it knows the way.

I was able to verify the journaled information mentioned above which brought back the memory of the spiritual impression. The confirmation happened about 6 months after looking at the journaling as I paid even closer attention to the information and outcomes. It was a powerful reminder to stay open and aware.

Responsibility

You are responsible for your spiritual gifts. You are responsible for using them for the good of all concerned. The good of all concerned includes you. You are responsible for what you say and when and to whom. There is a great responsibility when you are aware of your gift. Using your spiritual sensitivities to control, manipulate or otherwise deceive another is simply out of integrity and not spiritual at all.

Accountability and responsibility are crucial to your development as a human who has powerful and unique talents and skills, With great gifts and awareness comes great responsibility. Remaining in integrity and taking radical care of you is vital. You are responsible for your welfare and how you acknowledge and use your gifts.

Be aware of any potential liabilities that tag along with your intense sensitivities and seek connection with others as a way to moderate and navigate these situations.

Meet Joey

Joey is a business owner who has had a colorful past. He speaks about attitude and integrity as his top priorities. He acts in accordance with these principles at times and also comes out of integrity. When confronted about "intentionally creating unhealthy dependency" he smiles and responds, "I know, I like it that way."

Joey is a gifted person who also has spiritual sensitivities. He is able to tune in and use his ability to manipulate and control his employees and peers. Using charisma, he maneuvers through the workplace, setting up his agenda. His assistant later described this to me as gas lighting each person. Apparently, he was skilled and smiling on cue, overpaying the staff, and controlling behaviors with what appeared to be closeness. He also had a temper and would yell and threaten others.

Joey had spiritual sensitivities and he used them in ways that caused harm to many people. Using intuition and intensities for selfishness is not their intended use.

Joey continues his behaviors and apparently the only staff that remain are addicted to the financial security to their perception of the same. I share this story to offer an example of misuse of spiritual sensitivities. This is rampant in our society.

As an intensely sensitive person, you may run into this type of person, or you may have been tempted to use your connection in inauthentic ways. The damage and destruction that is left in this type of path is enormous for many reasons.

Energy and Frequency Sensitive

The dark side of being Gifted (Intensely Sensitive)

Many of the snippets below may reflect you or someone close to you. What I have learned over time is that many of our stories have similar threads. Here are a few events that you may find relatable.

In second grade, I came home crying about not fitting in with the other kids. I recall it had something to do with recess. I could not do the tumbling like others; I was afraid and embarrassed about my body. I was shy and introverted, already withdrawing. I crawled into my mother's lap and was telling her what happened. She hugged me and said, "Honey, you are different from the other kids, that's why they are doing these things." I interpreted this something "different" as something that was not measuring up or inherently flawed. It was decades later when I gained an understanding of what I now believe my mother was trying to say. She was attempting to comfort me, yet it was above my ability at the time to integrate into my understanding of self.

In 3rd grade, I was told by an art teacher that I was not the creative type. She critiqued my project and told me to focus on other things in life. Really? Third grade teacher telling a young child that they were not creative. Because I am gifted and intensely sensitive, this cut me to the core. I heard that I was not measuring up and never would. Intensely sensitive children are prone to assimilating others' comments even if they are unenlightened or wrong. I believed her and kept unknowingly reinforcing this idea for years. When I would decline all creative endeavors as I grew, no one could understand, the inner voice of not being good enough and not measuring up kept ringing in my head with her voice. Later, I was working with gifted creatives and had the opening to see the lie I believed and freed myself from that inner prison.

In 8th grade, then junior high school (grades 7-9), I was stabbed in the butt by some girls as I walked down the hall between classes. I had such low self-esteem and was so shut down that I told no one, especially my parents. I did not want to get into trouble. Someone told the principal, and I was called to the office the next day. I had never been in trouble, and this scared me to tears. The principal asked if it was true. I admitted that I was stabbed and described the girls. My parents were called in and they were shocked that I said nothing to them. They were unaware of the lack of safety in the home from my perspective. I honestly do not remember what happened after that day. I do remember feeling ashamed and embarrassed that I was the victim of a stabbing.

In high school I called the newly established Helpline as the family was violent all around me due to alcoholism and anger outbursts. It took everything I had to dial that number, shaking, and crying, desperate for some help. This had become a pattern and I was crumbling. When they answered, they put me on hold. I was never listened to or really heard. After a time, a woman came on and said,

"We cannot help you." Then the line disconnected. Message: You are not valuable enough to be listened to. No one wants to hear you. I was left feeling even more alone and isolated. This compounded the years of escalating violence secondary to alcohol abuse by parents. I was convinced no one would believe me.

Being gifted and intensely sensitive played an all-important role in how life landed on me and how I moved into adolescence and adulthood. I was not understood. In fact, I was laughed at often. I was told I was like a miniature adult and had to be and act like an adult from an early age. Each incident added to the previous and there seemed to be no way out. I was an alien; I did not belong and that was that. My mom listened to all the neighbor kids and yet declined to listen to her own daughter. Halo effect? Alcoholism? Naivete? I do not assign malicious motives to any of the adults. I believe they did not know any better and had no awareness as to how their words and actions impacted others, particularly the children.

Being intensely sensitive added an extra layer to the dysregulation, despair, and trauma. My spiritual sensitivities were made fun of, so I hid and withdrew inward. By the time I was in 11th grade, I could barely utter my name to a new person.

I learned to medicate with food, stuffing the pain. I would escape while sailing by disconnecting while staring at the bow wake of the boat. I would become over competitive and developed the belief that I had to be twice as good as anyone else to break even. I even wrote this in my high school annual one year. Looking back, I was disconnected much of the time to cope.

I excelled in academia while secretly thinking I was an impostor and a fraud. I chose my profession so that no teenager would have to hurt like I was hurting. "Everyone needs someone to talk to who will listen.", I thought. I so desperately wanted to help others, so they did not have to experience this level of exquisite pain.

Life lands on you differently than others when you are intensely sensitive. Sometimes breathing was hard. The dissociation was prevalent in most of my life areas until I was able to seek help and support.

Over the years, I have done my personal work to heal and rectify the wounds and trauma. I continue this personal work today and will always be working on myself. Looking back, I understand the role being gifted and intensely sensitive played in these situations as well as the countless others. My heart is so compassionate that I want to help everyone who is suffering. I have had to learn healthy boundaries with this over the years. When I say, "I get you", I do.

With experience, education, intuition, and knowledge, my technically eclectic style of life allows for deep inner work, expansive spiritual development, intuitive discernment, and play. Today, I am joy filled even when I may be sad. I have learned to regulate my nervous system. I can be with others as they heal and grow while not losing myself. I am sensitive to bullying, misunderstanding, ignoring, gas lighting, infantilizing, and degradation. I support the intensities and spiritual sensitivities in all people.

Afterall, your spiritual sensitivities are your gateway to a fulfilled life. They bridge the spiritual and the physical. Your intensities add the spice and energy to move through life with passion and purpose.

Mastering the Art of Discomfort – Not Being Like Everyone Else

I was told the other day by a medical professional "You are an anomaly" while she proceeded to continue to fit me into the box to fit her computer check marks.

What if you don't fit into the boxes in the computer program? Do you get left behind and have to live with increasing physical pain that bleeds into your mental well-being? What now?

Pain, chronic pain, can be a real killer of vision and vitality. It wears you down over time. This is an all-too-common experience. You most likely have had times of pain and injury. Maybe some have been chronic with no real end in sight.

Have you ever awakened in the night asking, "Is this my life now? Should I resign myself to impaired mobility and grieve the loss of independent functioning? Where are my family and friends as I walk through this pain?"

With OEs and Sensitivities on high alert, you learn the art of mastering discomfort. Part of the discomfort is a sense of loneliness. Some people may run or distance themselves during uncomfortable times because they may not know what to do or not do. Loneliness in gifted and spiritually sensitive people offers many learning lessons. When you are learning to master discomfort, walking parts of your path alone and parts with others can offer comfort and support in new ways. It is ok to be alone and not lonely. Feelings of loneliness are also valid. Honor your experience, tell the truth to you and others, and be open to those who can and will be present with you in your discomfort.

After months of seeking and searching for someone to hear you, really hear you, you will find those people. They will hear you, understand your needs, and take focused action. The solution to your challenge or pain will be at hand and the suffering from that pain and discomfort will stop. You will gain knowledge, insight, wisdom, and a great appreciation for many things during any challenging time that you can now share with others when the occasion arises. You can take pains you have grown through and use them to inspire and assist others.

Here are a few things Intensely Sensitive people can develop:

Deeper inner honesty that comes from surrender and acceptance - With all disruptions comes an invitation for increased honesty. Honesty on an internal level is much deeper than telling the truth; rather it relates to connection to your inner essence and honoring that essence. When life surprises you with a disruption, you are being invited to delve within and emerge with a new level of inner honesty. You will begin to experience disruptions, losses, or challenges as the pathways through which greater personal honesty and understanding are born. This honesty is a deeper knowing and connection to your essence.

Allowing the grieving process to happen without it taking the wheel is a much-needed skill for intensely sensitive individuals. Grief is a conflicting mass of human emotion following any significant change in behavior. Thus, these intense emotions that may not make cognitive sense can incite overwhelm. Learning to dance with the process without being all consumed takes focus, discipline, and support from a trusted other. You cannot effectively grieve alone.

Grief often takes a full cycle of seasons to integrate. Your feelings and understanding and impressions are valid. You will know when you are successfully integrating the grief when you can be reminded and it does not change your current mood toward the pain. As healing happens, you may even feel gratitude in the face of the event as it afforded you opportunities that would have not existed otherwise.

Never rush your healing, it is an organic flow and process. With all grief, it takes what it takes. Every person and every situation are different. There is no wrong way to grieve.

Looking for the Joyful moments and the good within the discomfort. I have learned over time that whenever my emotions/intuition are screaming, that a major change is about to happen. I also have learned that nothing turns out like my gifted brain wants to believe. Life is always more thrilling and beautiful that our limited perceptions often try to tell us. Even when struggling, allow yourself to seek safe support so you will be heard, ride the waves, and then invite awareness of the good as you emerge on the other side.

Having intense sensitivities can be challenging. I use the mantra "I am constantly tripping over joyful moments." Even in discomfort and disruption, joy can be found when we allow room. It will appear at the right time. No need to attempt to push or force things to happen.

Receiving care, love, and support – Most sensitives give a lot to others over the years. Can you receive from others? Receiving is as important and maybe more important than giving to others. Interestingly some support comes from different people than you might have thought. Still, practice receiving in a humble manner. This is of great benefit for you and others in the long run.

Note that when you block someone from giving to you in a healthy manner, you are blocking their good and your good. It is not noble to deflect a compliment or a kind word. It blocks both the giver and the receiver.

Deeper Inner Spiritual Connection – As you listen more acutely to your inner self or spirit, you will have a knowingness of what is good for you, really. The deeper you develop your inner connection, the more peaceful and focused you become. This connection transcends words, ideology, dogma, and intellectual prowess. First you develop an open minded and open-hearted mindset and allow your Higher Self to emerge. You keep evolving and growing from there.

Over time, your deeper connection will grow in ways that will surprise you. Your will have great experiences as well as confounding experiences and understandings. Eventually, it all begins to come together. Where there is paradox, you will notice that there is a spiritual truth, lesson, or understanding emerging. It may seem unsettling initially. Sit and pay attention. Verify and confirm as time moves forward. The higher purpose will always be revealed. It may not be what you think, This is where inner honesty ad connection to your essence is valuable.

Honoring you and your diversity – Do not try to fit into a box that others construct - you may end up paying a negative price. It never, ever works out well. Keep going until you are heard and treated with respect which includes your diverse make-up. Your unique intense make-up transcends words and paradigms. Remember that the paradigms are simply pointing to the experience, they are not the experience.

Our brains tell us that everyone thinks alike and experiences the world the same when in fact, no one thinks alike or experiences the world the same. We are all diverse, not some of us. We are diverse in biology, neurology, autobiography, sensitivities, and intensities in addition to other environmental factors.

New levels of understanding and compassion for the suffering and challenges of others. You can use your intense sensitivities in your favor with focus. Your deep connection and ability to feel into places and situations affords you a unique and powerful opportunity to serve others, simply by being present and taking the right action.

The more you develop your inner gifts and sensitivities, the more you will see opportunities to connect within and thus connect with others along your path. These connections are vital for our sense of well-being.

There are many other skills and talents that an intensely sensitive person develops over time. As you embrace your personal connection to self and nature, you will discover wonder and beauty just waiting for you to say yes!

You may feel some trepidation along the way or have lots of questions. This is where a mentor is valuable. A mentor has specific experience with the questions you are asking. The key for you is to have an open mind. Einstein said, "You cannot solve a problem with the same thinking that created it." Gifted people are taught that everything can be figured out cognitively. This is not the case. Often your intuition (highest form of intelligence) can lead to your greater understanding and then your linear mind can go from there.

Ultimately, you will develop an amazing balance and marriage of your giftedness, intensities, spiritual sensitivities, autobiography, and personality to create a beautiful life that is worthy of signing autographs! Yes, it takes focused action to yield positive results and it is worth every part of your investment.

Points to Ponder:

1. With which one or combination of overexcitabilities do you most resonate?

2. How do your spiritual sensitivities manifest in your life?

3. Are your intensities your ally or your foe? What does this mean to you?

4. Where are the people who understand you? Do you interact with them and share your authentic experience?

5. How do intense sensitivities (yours or anothers') impact your life?

6. Do you listen and support others who are intensely sensitive?

Chapter V.

Standing in Your Personal Authority

No one belongs here more than you.

~~ Brené Brown

You have a right to be here. Personal Authority is about knowing who you are and what you offer while standing in this Truth. You are here with many gifts that are meant to be offered. You, and only you, can be and do your personal mission. Whether you are aware of it or not, you are here on purpose with a purpose. With all your intense sensitivities, gifts, and talents, you are truly equipped to stand in your personal authority.

Do not mistake this as an ego trip on being better than or superior. Personal authority is being your authentic self, using your unique gifts to humbly serve. Often when you hear the word authority, you may think of controlling or an abrupt nature. Personal Authority from an inclusive spiritual perspective means that you are allowing your authentic nature to emerge from within with humility, compassion, and kindness.

When you stand in this place, you attract others of like mind. Your inner creativity and flow come alive. Your intense sensitivities serve you more deeply and your understanding brings a sense of inner peace.

Personal Sovereignty

Personal sovereignty is a form of self-ownership. It shows up in your life as healthy, respectful boundaries that beautifully balance your personal needs and desires with those around you with respect and grace.

You may have been taught to put others in front of yourself. There are times when this may be true and on an inner level, you want to learn to keep your resource tank full and freely give from your overflow. This requires healthy outer and inner boundaries, radical self-care that is a daily action. Self-care in response to being tired or spent is really recovery and these are not the same thing.

Changing and evolving beyond your old beliefs and constructs can be challenging and offer grand lessons, insights, and experiences. Claiming your personal authority or sovereignty means that attempts to control or manipulate you are unsuccessful. You make your own decisions and choose who you are in relationship with and how you navigate your inner and outer worlds. Your natural presence enters any room even before you are visibly seen. This presence is often indescribable for others. They are connected with your inner sense of sovereignty and self-worth.

The value in being you and standing your ground with ease and grace is that your presence, not your ego, is present and engaged in life. Some of my clients have been concerned about their egos getting in the way. This is why we have trusted others and are developing continuously. I often say to myself, "Am I evolving or devolving?".

Your boundaries will be tested by others. As you develop your sense of personal authority, your "yes" will be yes and your "no" will be no. The more authentically aligned and clear you remain, the more respect you develop in your relationships.

Meet Mary

Mary is a successful businesswoman. She excels in her profession and has made a name for herself within her industry. Mary is amazing and talented. Mary has a great sense of humor, and she uses it often. She is serious about business though. Mary has many places of interest, and she devotes herself fully to each of these interests while she is engaged.

Mary shared with me that many of her life struggles have come from not being understood, particularly regarding her sense of humor. Because she uses words differently than many others, she has had some difficulty with interpersonal connections.

Mary and I worked together in workshops as well as individual and business arenas. She began to develop insights into her sensitivities and her giftedness. Mary denied any of her valuable differences, intensities, and sensitivities at first. She could see the intense sensitivities in her other family members, but not herself. This type of blind spot is typical. You often do not see aspects of yourself as unique when you have been living with them all your life, right? As Mary began to open her mind to the possibilities, she was able to begin to see how she has excelled and how she has struggled over her life.

After some time and some honoring and self-development, Mary now can stand in her personal authority without personalizing others' reactions. Mary is now able to share her experience and awareness and knowledge with others from a place of inner authority and knowing. These gifts and sensitivities are being used by Mary to uplift herself and those around her.

Underachieving

You may be thinking that you or a loved one is an underachiever. Did you know that underachieving can be an indicator not only of giftedness but of any of the overexcitabilities or intensities? Many sensitives that I know have struggled in school and at various stages throughout their lives.

They heard often that they are too smart to be failing or being disruptive. This is precisely the point. For bright and sensitive people, when boredom sets in, all bets are off. Some will find something to meet their curiosity drive and comply with the system at hand. Others may get bored and within the boredom is the potential for disruption, thus underachieving.

I have met gifted and talented people who have great sensitivities who are doing manual labor or have moved to remote areas to get away from the expectations and challenges in "the real world". This is a form of underachieving or underemployment. It can be perpetuated by the society at large or by belief systems within the person or both.

Still, underachieving can be a sign that you are bright, intense, AND sensitive in ways that you do not yet understand or want to bring out into the world. Some underachievers I have worked with report negative, even traumatic, experiences regarding their achievements when they were young, so they checked out of realizing their vision or heart's desire at an early age. This dissociating from your inherent inner calling can cause depression, anxiety and many other significant challenges including addiction in one form or another.

Your inner vision is still within you and is always inviting you to express it in your world. The more you try to ignore or avoid your inner vision, the more it reminds you that it is there. When you try to avoid listening within your vision or calling, look at your life and see what keeps showing up. Here is your answer!

Your small-minded ego may then say, "How am I to do this?" and send you into a fear and procrastination loop. Your answer now is: "I may not know how, and still, my answer is Yes. I am willing to follow my inner vision and I trust the path will unfold perfectly." It is within your momentum and actions that your life opens before you.

Starting and stopping makes everything seem more difficult. Think of a boat and its rudder. Without momentum, the rudder which steers the boat is useless. With momentum, the rudder can now guide the boat easier. By taking reasonable actions, you keep your momentum going and it makes your adjustments along the way much more fluid. Keep moving and adjust accordingly.

Points to Ponder:

1. What does personal authority mean to you?

2. What is your demeanor when you are living in your authentic strength?

3. How does your personal sovereignty feel?

4. How would you be even more amazing as you own your intensities?

Chapter VI.

Inner Integrity

Stop looking for something out there and begin seeing within.

~~ *Rumi*

When you possess acute reasoning, intense and profound emotions, visionary imagination, and intellectual prowess, looking within may seem a bit daunting. Your fears and apprehension may be related to your ability or understanding of how to make friends with you or anyone else for that matter. Intensity requires connection to thrive. If you ever have the opportunity to hear me speak at an event, you will often hear me talk about connection being the correction.

Looking within is the most vital and important connection for your success, satisfaction, and happiness. If you have been living from your intellect and solving every problem with the scientific method, you are missing out on a significant part of your sensitivities that can help you navigate this insensitive world more effectively. Your inner connection will always offer you guidance and direction on what most aligns with your calling or vision. When you stray from your authentic path, the pain of separation can take hold and undermine your confidence, self-esteem, and happiness.

It is vital that you take time to look within. This takes inner quiet and a willingness to touch your inner Truth. From this still place within you can bring your gifts to the world with integrity and authenticity. I am most quiet within when I am walking in nature, swimming or sailing. You can be quiet within while moving your body. In fact, many people with physical intensities find moving helps them go within. Do what works for you and be willing to experiment.

There are many ways to deepen your inner connection. Walking in nature and focusing on the natural world in gratitude, cooking a new recipe, paying attention to your breathing while driving or sitting, journaling your ideas, drawing, or creating art of any kind, moving your body in dance or exercise, and honoring how you experience the movement, and contemplation of all kinds are all great ways to continue to deepen your connection.

Connection Exercise

Here are steps to assist you in connecting with your Inner Truth:

✓ Put down all distractions and turn off alarms, buzzers, bells, and notifications.

✓ Have stillness, inner quiet or ambient music.

✓ Close your eyes or gaze at a candle flame.

✓ Exhale for the count of 4 or 6, whichever is most comfortable.

✓ When your air is completely released, pause for 2 seconds.

✓ Allowing air to fill your lungs to the count of 4 or 6. Pause.

✓ Release the air. Keeping your exhale and inhales about the same duration. Always pausing for 2 seconds.

✓ Allow your thoughts to float through your consciousness like puffy clouds. Releasing the need to hold on or follow them.

✓ Ask yourself: "What is mine to do?".

✓ Sit with this idea and listen to your inner prompting. You may hear something or have an impression. Allow the prompting to hang out with you and feel your resonance with the messages.

✓ Release any fear or apprehension.

✓ Keep paying attention.

✓ Stay in this open and receptive place, breathing for about 15-20 minutes.

✓ When you are done, write down what came to you without judgment. Simply transcribe what you thought, felt, or heard.

I suggest a special journal where these times of quiet reflection can be documented.

✓ Do this daily. After 20-30 days, re-read your journal entries.

✓ Look for themes that are emerging.

✓ You will begin to see your path clearly.

You may be saying that you do not want to or can't sit still. Notice that I said inner quiet. For intensely sensitive people, your body may need to be moving to reach an inner quiet. This is perfectly acceptable. Remember part of being intensely sensitive means that you may experience things differently than others. Different is not better or worse.

You can use your body's movement to help quiet within. Running, swimming, walking, or cycling in rhythm to a mental cadence can help you reach an inner quiet. This is where the magic and beauty of your intense sensitivities come together for inspiration, creativity, and awesomeness.

Meet Peter

Peter struggles with looking within. He is a sensitive and intense smart man who often denies his inner pain with humor and a gregarious personality. Peter is talented and he experiences things vividly. Peter is stuck in his head, and he must intellectually understand things before getting to a place of acceptance.

I have worked with Peter on the idea that not all things can be understood intellectually that some aspects of life are not meant for intellectual understanding. There are emotions and life mysteries that defy cognitive reasoning. Peter will admit to this, yet he continues to overthink and rationalize his life.

Peter has received many wake-up calls to help him acknowledge and develop his giftedness, intensities, and sensitivities. Peter appears open mentally yet has not taken authentic action toward opening to the idea that there is more to his giftedness and his intensities than being a fast thinker. He sometimes denies this part of himself.

We have spoken numerous times about these aspects of life and Peter seems to continue his fast-mental pace without ever slowing down and looking within. This has caused problems within his family, marriage, work, and physical health. Still, Peter runs from himself.

Fear is what stops him from looking within. Fear of losing something or not getting something. Maybe even the fear that others have had a point all along! Peter has stated that he is going to start to look within by meditating and being quieter inwardly. If Peter does not learn skills to be quieter and look within, Peter's life challenges will continue and even become worse. Looking within and being willing to be with yourself is a vital part of living a productive, successful, and wise life. Peter is resisting, he is also paying the consequences. He is experiencing digestion issues, anxiety, sleep problems, and some relational disconnections.

Having information and third-party input is fine. There is nothing wrong with that. There does, however, come a time when the blame, external focus, and distractions must stop long enough to go within and see what is there. Others can travel the road with you and yet you, and only you, can walk your personal path.

Peter is like many - afraid that he may not like what he will find. Letting fear keep you from your vision is a sad, painful place to live. I want more for Peter, and he must be the one to take the proper actions. There is no vicarious atonement. Everyone must do their own inner work to free themselves of inner distortions or outdated beliefs and behaviors.

Points to Ponder:

1. Are you comfortable being quiet?

2. How do you achieve your inner quiet zone?

3. Are you fearful of what you might hear within if you are quiet?

4. Where in nature do you find solace? Do you frequent this location?

5. Where does your creativity shine most?

CHAPTER VII.

Opening to Possibilities

Don't be pushed by your problems, be led by your dreams.
                              ~~Ralph Waldo Emerson

There is a great pull between intense sensitivities and wanting to be numb. Being open to possibilities is a great way to further acknowledge and appreciate your inner gifts and intensities. First and foremost, relax; it is going to be okay! Being open to possibilities is all about relaxing into the amazing wealth of ideas, visions, and opportunities that abound. You are swimming in infinite possibilities, whether you realize this or not.

Intensely sensitive people can "see" solutions and have ideas that others don't experience. Being open to the abundant possibilities uses your sensitivities to offer solutions and ideas for the greater good. Most likely, your intense sensitivities also enable you to see potential challenges or blocks in advance. This ability is useful on all levels and can be especially useful in business. Many intense sensitives own or manage businesses. These abilities enable you to be able to guide and direct the team by asking insightful questions that can bring to light solutions for challenges before they appear.

Possibilities are endless. Going within, your depth and awareness can bring forth inspiring solutions and outcomes. Expanding your focus outward, possibilities abound in and through all situations and people. The key is to be open. You may be tempted to judge things by appearances. You see and experience everything through your autobiography. You may be conditioned to rule out certain things that could now serve you. Being open and paying attention can assist you in making even more progress toward living comfortably in an insensitive world. Just because something wasn't right for you years ago doesn't necessarily mean the same today. Be open.

In workshops and individual meetings with clients, we remain focused on being open to possibilities and opportunities, especially those that show up in unexpected ways. There have been times when I had an inspired idea and then as I continued the workshop, realized that the idea resonated with a participant. Being open, I shared the inspired idea with the participant on a break. Come to find out, it aligned with her new business model that she had not unveiled at the time. She interpreted my comments as an affirmation of her direction. Being open to possibilities for both of us in that moment was essential to progress and success for her.

Contempt prior to investigation is one of the ways you may hold yourself back and keep your intensities firing needlessly. You may be quick to access or judge some opportunities. It will serve you better to remain open and try on the opportunity, really. Check in with yourself on how options feel to you rather than only thinking. Comparison to others or your past is not always the most aligned or authentic way to approach your life. Even ruling things out because of your uncertainty of the future can hold you back and add frustration and needless stress to your daily life. Be open and pay attention to how things feel. Here is a great key for your peace of mind and your successful fulfillment.

To be open to your possibilities means just this. Be open, mentally open, emotionally open, physically open, socially open, and spiritually open and be attentive as to allow your vision to emerge with your intense sensitivities offering you the fuel for the journey. When any life area is closed because of fear, doubt, pain, grief or worry, you may be suffering from some level of dissatisfaction or underachievement.

Allowing your intensities to offer you the fuel, you can navigate this insensitive world using your sensitivities as your gift rather than a liability. Being intensely sensitive in an insensitive world can be challenging if you get distracted by others or allow their energy to grab you. Instead, be open to the possibilities within any situation or interaction and follow your guided opportunities and bright ideas.

You will then feel more confident and the insensitivity around you won't be able to gain the momentum to distract or stop your vision.

Meet Karla

Karla is a gifted and intensely sensitive businesswoman. Her career spans decades and everything she works on works well. She has worked with me on various levels to determine how to better use her skills and for overall personal development. Karla is a kind-hearted person.

Karla can see business challenges and opportunities before they are obvious to others. Her ability to listen to a strategy and see potential outcomes and obstacles is uncanny. Karla has shared that she has used this skill and other businesspeople either ignored her or otherwise negated her input. Because she is intensely sensitive, she felt the emotional pain deeply. Over time, she has learned to "keep my mouth shut" as she told me.

Stifling or squashing your intensities and giftedness can cause problems in many areas of your life. From physical health challenges to some misunderstandings with business colleagues, Karla has become more reserved when it comes to her input regarding business and strategy. She is protecting her feelings while avoiding the responses from others.

As Karla became friends with this aspect of her inner self, she has begun to see even more possibilities for her business and the business of others. Karla uses her ability and willingness to be open to possibilities and therefore propel her vision into reality. She also is highly sought after for her insights in the business world.

By being open to possibilities, Karla is paving the way to greater success than she initially imagined. She also will enjoy the journey more with much less doubt, worry or fear.

Obstacles

Obstacles to being open can be formidable. It is important for you to pay attention to your intense sensitivities and allow them to be acknowledged and valued. You may have known obstacles and unknown obstacles that are in your unconscious or blind spots. Sometimes the most motivated people have some unconscious resistance to change that can create interesting challenges.

Fear is an obstacle. The function of fear is to get ready or get prepared. Many people recoil at the feeling of fear or try to pretend it is not happening. Fear has nothing to do with weakness. Fear tells you to get yourself ready for what is coming. Fear is not just feeling afraid. Fear comes looking like anxiety or nervousness at times and analysis paralysis at other times. Still the message remains, get ready.

Worry is another obstacle. Worry is focusing too much on the future uncertainties. The future is not guaranteed. Be more present today. Do what you can today with what you have. Have faith that your actions today will keep your momentum going so you can navigate the twists and turns of life effectively.

I always tell myself, "Worry means praying for something to go wrong". I remind myself that whatever I am focusing my energy and attention toward is where I am heading. Most things I could worry about are not in alignment with my highest calling. Worry lacks good stewardship of our most valuable resources, time, attention, and energy.

Doubt is a dream killer. I always tell my clients (and me sometimes) that if the bright idea is yours then the Universe will assist your journey. We all have different visions and missions. Your intensities are your booster rockets to help propel you even farther than you can imagine before lift-off! We all have our unique ideas and heart's desires. Your biggest mistake is when you take on someone else's great idea and try to make it your own. Therefore, the people who try to live the dreams their parents scripted for them are usually unhappy or may even sabotage their success. Follow your own inner guidance, pay attention to feedback and timing. Release doubt and say yes to your inner promptings. Your path will be made clear as you get moving.

Creativity Wounds are prevalent in gifted and talented people. These happen when the creator receives negative or cautionary input about their creation. The idea of "the starving artist" comes from this wound. Your creative genius will come through when you allow it to emerge. Your inner essence is connected to your creations, so they are sacred. When someone shares their creation with you, honor that creation. By doing so, you honor them.

When you restrict your creativity by comparison, self-consciousness or believing someone else's comments, you allow that wound to fester. These old wounds interfere with our intense sensitivities and our inherent connection. Just because your 3rd grade teacher said you are not creative does not make it true.

Life static is another obstacle. Becoming too busy or allowing too much inner or outer noise to create static in your life. You know this is happening when simple things seem more difficult or hard to get accomplished. You may even notice you sigh often and may have thoughts that are increasingly pessimistic.

Sometimes life static can consist of avoidance and distractions that are simple time stealers. Remember that you have so much energy for each day and to spend your energy on distractions may not be your best choice. Static comes when our undisclosed motive is avoidance or another form of chaos or confusion.

Grief is a conflicting mass of human emotion following any significant change in behavior. Grief can be an obstacle when we remain stuck or holding on to the grief we may be feeling. There is great energy in your emotions. Spend time with them and be curious about how you can use their energy for your highest good as a beneficial presence on this planet. There is always a noble use of your energy available. The question is whether you will seize the opportunity or not.

Blind Spots are not something to be ashamed of or deny. Everyone has blind spots; spots where our own awareness ends yet others can see. Blind spots have an important role in our development as spiritually intense beings. They contain a treasure trove of information and opportunity for development and expansion.

When we run up against a blind spot, it may not always feel great. It may even feel down right upsetting, painful or annoying. Yet, within these emotions is a nugget of Joy and wisdom awaiting our awareness and ownership. When I began to make friends with my blind spots, and everyone has them, I became much freer to learn and grow from the inside out. Fear and expectation lost their grip on my psyche.

Possibilities

There are many possibilities, and you can think of many more than you initially might realize! Your limited, though genius and intense brains cannot possibly consider ALL the possibilities. I have created some groups of possibilities to offer you some inspiration for your vision. This is not exhaustive. Add your own groupings as you wish. These are meant to serve to prime your inner possibility pump!

Explorers – Question Askers

Curious George would be here. Always asking questions, seeking within and without. Some explorers explore the outer realms like space, the ocean, wilderness, and the like. The inner explorers are always asking questions that are focused on the inner realms like biology, DNA, quantum physics, string theory, spirituality, meaning and purpose. Some explorers become excited to varying degrees. I work with many people who are explorers in one way or another. Some are spiritual seekers, and some are scientists, yet they are all explorers. I think this may be part of why they work with me; their natural propensity to ask questions, ponder and explore new ideas and realms.

Many question askers start at an early age. Being inquisitive is a creative gift that helps grow consciousness and it shows up in many iterations. Some are scientists who are exploring neurology, biology, genetics, space and more. Some explorers are archaeologists who are digging into civilizations past while current day explorers can be deep sea diving, heading into the wilderness, or heading into space.

Language Lovers and Storytellers

This group of possibilities include the great storytellers and lovers of language. Many bright and sensitive people use language differently than others. Their sense of humor uses unusual use of words and ideas. You may be a great oral storyteller or maybe a great poet or writer. You may have an affinity and love for great literature. You may even want to learn or already know multiple languages. All these types of possibilities are natural for those of you who have a natural love of language and story.

Using metaphors in teaching and illustrating ideas is a sure sign of the language lover. Many storytellers take vast or complicated concepts and distill them down into terms and presentation that is accessible and meaningful for others. My grandmother and mother loved language. I was taught from an early age to use words with precision and know the meaning of the words you use. What were you taught directly or indirectly about language and the use of words?

The Love of Numbers and Calculating

Math and arithmetic folks land in this group. The love of geometry, sacred geometry, and number patterns can be seen in this group. I have a client who can calculate figures for his business so rapidly it seems like he has memorized static numbers. Yet, when you listen, he is doing the calculating as he speaks. You may be like this client, or your love of numbers may show up in entirely different ways. I know accountants and investment people who love to talk figures while non-number lovers may be bored or not interested. Remember, there is no better than or worse than. These are ideas of groups of possibilities.

I love numbers and seeing patterns in numbers as I go through the day. I am paying attention to how numbers feel in various situations. For example, the number of my new home address adds up to 22 which is a number that has followed me throughout my life. This realization felt great as I made my offer for the purchase of the home. Numbers play an important role in varied ways.

Numbers are also important in the technical aspect of music and music production. Numbers and calculating are paramount in research and presenting research findings. This group of possibilities is vast and covers lots of territory.

Playful Muses

Play and fun sometimes get a bad rap. Play and being lighthearted are vital to your conscious creativity and access to many possibilities. Muses are those who find joy in play often bring a much-needed levity to any situation. Within play and fun are creative ideas just waiting to be birthed.

When I catch myself becoming too serious or focused to the point of damaging stress, I consciously lighten my point of reference and give myself permission to play and laugh. This pattern interrupt serves my creative genius and relaxes my intensities. My sensitivities and intuition have a chance to come through and be heard. This is an essential balance for my ongoing life's work and vision.

Learning to use play effectively is important. Some people may play as an avoidant behavior. This is a misplaced use of their muse. I love to see your muse come out to play even in the midst of serious work and achievement. Sometimes your inner landscape can have play while your work is focused and precise.

Connectors - Bring People Together

Connectors are those who have the natural gifts and talent to bring people together. They are always introducing people to other people, ideas, and opportunities. They can't seem to help themselves. I know a connector who is introducing and sharing people with other people. She often laughs because she doesn't know why she thinks of introducing certain folks, but she does it anyway. Many great connections and adventures have been born through her connecting possibilities.

Being a connector can come in many forms. Some connect data points in research or academia while others may connect people and network with fluidity. Many of the connectors I know enjoy connecting ideas, people and like interests. They report a sense of fulfillment or accomplishment.

Inventors, Scientists and Developers

Do you like to invent things? Do you enjoy exploring the sciences? I love chemistry and physics. I even studied celestial navigation and was fascinated by the solar system and navigating using this age-old skill. I find the engineer type mind that can often be a great specialist in this possibility group.

There are people who can be a specialist in multiple areas. I know folks who have several successful inventions. I have worked with scientists who have excelled in multiple areas within the field they study. Here you will identify your inquisitive mind that also loves to experiment and gather valuable information used in forming thesis statements and conclusions to questions.

Leadership and People Magnets

Visionary leaders are another common group I work with day to day. Leadership and management are different from control. Good leaders are emotionally stable and have excellent discernment skills. They are people magnets naturally. In any group, the leadership-oriented people have people around them because others are naturally drawn to them. This possibility has many variations. I have a client who has this possibility, and he is angry often due to unhealed wounds. He sets his limits and boundaries with an angry and controlling tone even though that is not his intention. We work on this balance and ways to let the leadership possibility flourish while diminishing the impact and disruption of the old grief and fear.

Another professional naturally has people around her and she also has undisclosed motives at times. She is developing strategies to cease the undisclosed motive so her authentic motives and desires can come through more fully. Both people and others have leadership possibilities. Watch any group that has a crisis or challenge. The person that will be called upon for leadership will be the person with this leadership possibility. This may or may not be the leader by position.

Artistic Visionaries – Art, Music, and Movement

My mother had this possibility. She played the piano and was a great sketch artist. She would sketch clothing designs that just naturally came to her. She did not see the beauty and value in her artistic possibilities. She also taught dance with my father. My brother and I would tag along and dance too! My mother had this possibility on all levels. Sadly, she kept much of this gift to herself, never realizing her dreams which caused her great grief and most likely was the fuel for her medicating away the pain of not allowing the intense sensitivities to fully emerge.

I work with many artistic people. They have talents in many areas. The more they allow their transformation and expression of their possibilities, the happier and more satisfied they become. It is all in the healthy expression of your intense sensitivities that helps you thrive in this insensitive world. Your intensities have within them the fuel to propel you toward your vision regardless of the others around you. It takes trust and focus to bring your creations to life. This is where good accountability and support can be beneficial.

Athletes – Movement with Purpose

Athletes that have this amazing possibility often excel in their sport. They have an uncanny way of being able to simply know what to do and can anticipate their opponent's next move. It comes so naturally that some athletes do not understand why others have to work differently to achieve similar performance levels. Many athletes see life as a competition, and they must learn the finesse of using their intense sensitivities in a fluid manner. I always point to the great running backs in football like Emmitt Smith and Barry Sanders. They ran with finesse, talent and a skill that was a step above other players. They seemed almost magical in their movements and how they knew what was coming. It is their intense sensitivity that afforded them the possibility to excel. Still, they had to put in the diligent work, focused action, and massive determination to reach the pinnacle of their careers.

Athletes must also be prepared to use their intensities after the game or sports career has concluded. Many of them struggle because they do not consider what's next and they get stuck. I work with athletes to help them use their intense sensitivities for continued success rather than creating their demise.

The Five Essentials

In my book *Where Do You Fit In?* I share 5 essentials and how these essential gifts can work together when acknowledged and appreciated for their unique roles in relationships.

The 5 Essentials are:

1. **The Baller** is dialed into the relentless source of energy.

2. **The Weaver** bridges ideas and concepts with a creative and spiritual flow.

3. **The Harmonizer** is playful and lighthearted, smoothing rough edges of the group.

4. **The Worker** are the stabilizers who are goal oriented.

5. **The Creator** is connected to purpose and intention.

The book speaks to each of these essential gifts and shares how to make noise, using your essential nature to serve you and others in a meaningful manner. The book is available wherever books are sold.

Regardless of how you identify and relate to your inner gifts and emerging possibilities, it is vital that you invest in yourself by making friends with and fostering development of your inner treasure trove of gifts that are uniquely combines in you,

Now is the time to connect in an open manner with the possibilities above or another you identify for yourself. Using your intense sensitivities, where are you drawn? How are these possibilities showing up in your life? In what life areas are they asking to be brought forth to emerge?

Feel your excitement and the energy of allowing your possibilities to express themselves. Your empowerment and enthusiasm can and will give you what you need to move forward in ways more amazing than you can see now.

Points to Ponder:

1. What does "being open" mean to you?

2. What obstacles do you identify in your life now?

3. Do you have a sense of more abundant possibilities than you can see right now?

4. How do you respond to the folks who cannot "see" what you see?

5. Document several possibilities you can see now and check back in 30 days to see your progress and success!

Chapter VIII.

Your Intrinsic Wealth

To have a sense of one's intrinsic worth which constitutes self-respect is potentially to have anything.

~~ *Joan Didion*

You are swimming in richness and abundance on all levels. Your intensities are a form of wealth. You experience life with a wealth of depth and vibrancy that others may miss. You have a wealth of inspired ideas, a wealth of emotion, a wealth of energy, a wealth of possible connections, and a wealth of life experience.

How are you harnessing and focusing your wealth? Are you letting it drain away like sand through a sieve? Or are you driving the team of strong Clydesdales as they use their power and strength to pull you toward your vision and destination. To use your skills to focus and steer your intense sensitivities toward your goals takes training and patience.

You simply don't wake up one day knowing how to drive the team of intense sensitivities. And your intense sensitivities must be trained to work together and respond to your directions. Using our example of a team of Clydesdales – each one is powerful, strong, and determined. Your skill is in directing these characteristics, not in trying to squelch or stop them. You must learn to tune in, be patient and act from a state of inner flow. Forcing or pushing is not effective.

As your team begins to interact and work together, they can be harnessed; thus, using each one's strength to work in concert with the team. Your intensities and sensitivities are much the same. They are all connected and when focused on a common goal, quite powerful.

Meet Molly

Molly is a college student who has many intense sensitivities. She has had some challenges with focusing her thoughts and actions. When we speak, she shares that her intense sensitivities seem more like a curse than a gift at times. She considers herself a geek because she loves chemistry and calculus, she also considers herself an athlete because she is on the swim team. Molly also enjoys visual arts, and she paints great paintings. She straddles these worlds, and her intense sensitivities allow her to excel. Molly says she likes being intensely sensitive when she wants to excel and is not so fond of her intense sensitivities when she wants to chill and relax with some girlfriends. Molly finds that her intensities are often alive and forefront even when she wants a break.

When we discussed her inherent wealth, she said she could understand what I was saying but she did not get how the boy she was recently dating told her that he wanted to be friends because she was so intense and so sensitive. He thought she could see through him, and it made him nervous. "How is this inherent wealth?" she asked with a tense tone. If this is wealth, I think I want to be poor. Then she laughed and said, "not really".

Over time, Molly practiced riding the waves rather than trying to control the waves. As she loved the beach, this visual was familiar. Swimming in the ocean to practice, she could feel the lesson in riding the waves rather than attempting to force an outcome. Harnessing her inherent wealth of moving energy in her mind, emotions and body took some time. I believe it is a great life practice to manage your wealth and be a good steward. This includes your inner wealth. Your vital energy that tells you that you are alive, the energy that propels you toward your goal.

Molly continued to focus on managing and directing her intense sensitivities rather than stuffing them or trying to pretend they aren't there and thus creating depression and anxiety. She manages her emotional intensities by using breathing, mindfulness, and meditation in several forms. She has learned self-soothing with calming teas, warm baths, and weighted blankets for sleep. She manages her intellectual intensities by allowing her curiosity time to play and setting limits on her time of investigation. Molly manages her physical wealth of intensity by participating in competitive sport and allowing herself to be active as a form of connection and self-care.

Molly has learned to establish and maintain multiple peer groups to help fulfill her varied social, intellectual, spiritual, emotional, and physical needs. With multiple peer groups, Molly can now get her needs met more efficiently by matching the need to the group and accessing that particular group for support or engagement. She talks to her geeky friends about things they have in common, so she feels satisfied. She can then enjoy girlfriend nights of relaxation because the other needs for connection are fulfilled. It becomes a nice equilibrium when Molly has people she is connected to on various levels in each group.

With more life satisfaction, Molly can now more fully enjoy her inherent wealth of intensities and sensitivities on all levels.

When you see yourself as inherently wealthy and abundant, you interact with life differently than someone who is coming from a poverty mentality. The truth is that you are here on Earth, fully equipped and fully able to do what ought to be done by you. Your vision is uniquely yours and you have all the resources needed to fulfill your vision in style. Your role is to say yes and act along these lines.

Your intense sensitivities afford you a unique perspective in life. You, my friend, are here on purpose with a mighty purpose.

Points to Ponder:

1. Define wealth.

2. How do you express your inherent inner wealth?

3. What blocks your connection to your wealth? What can clear the blocks?

4. Do you know you are inherently wealthy? What is your evidence?

5. How can you use your inherent wealth to manifest your vision?

CHAPTER IX.

Allow Connection

Connection is why we are here. We are hardwired to connect with others, it's what gives meaning and purpose to our lives, and without it, there is suffering.

~~ *Brené Brown*

Connection is vital to our welfare. Humans are pack animals and thus we require connection to thrive. We must allow authentic connection to thrive. I always think of some forms of intimacy when I think of connection. Intimacy can be understood as In-To-Me-See. You must be willing to look within and connect to your inherent value as a human being sucking air. Connection also extends to others and the natural world.

Three Types of Connection

There are three types of connection that are central to happiness and success for intense sensitives. Each one interfaces with the others. These types of connections work in harmony for overall life fulfillment.

The first type is connection with others. Who in your life "gets you?" Can you be fully present and connected to those around you? Connection refers to a meeting of heart, mind, and soul. This is deeper than superficial interactions. There are various types of connection with varying intensities. This makes life interesting and rewarding. Often, we are taught to try to make everything the same, this will not work for an intensely sensitive person who requires diversity to thrive.

The second type of connection is connection to your inner (Higher) self. This is often referred to as intuition, gut feelings, or inspired ideas. Are you connected to and paying attention to your inspiration?

The third type is connection to the Universe at large. How aware are you of your vital and necessary role in the Universe? You, with all your intense sensitivities are here to affect an uplifting impact in the Universe. This concept of Unity with all is also the cornerstone in Yoga practice. Our connection to all that expands far beyond our limited human brain can comprehend, even for gifted people.

Allowing connection in each of these areas means to breathe and relax into who you are and your special role. This experience is the opposite from pushing and forcing ideas and agendas.

To allow means to be open to a flow that serves you and others, a flow of equilibrium and mutual positive regard. When you put your walls up or engage only from your prefrontal cortex, you are missing a large part of connection.

Authentic connection is an experience that brings ultimate fulfillment and is very difficult to describe in words. If you have ever had a connection where time seemed to stand still or was irrelevant, you have experienced a deep level of connection.

Meet Bryant

Bryant is uniquely qualified in the medical chemotherapy world. He has education and expertise that physicians and specialists seek on a daily basis. Bryant also has great intuitive insights that complement his intellectual prowess. Bryant works in a medical facility where there are primarily women coworkers. He enjoys his work and loves solving complex biological and chemical problems. He is an introvert who doesn't like small talk and typically avoids these types of encounters.

Bryant isolates often and has had bouts of existential depression. He loves to read and study. He finds little interest in loud places or events. The depression he describes as "being able to see solutions in some medical problems and when he tries to engage colleagues, they dismiss him." He reports that he has insights and can see solutions that others don't see until about a year has passed. This disconnection from colleagues has caused him sadness and some loneliness at work.

In fact, Bryant sought his EAP counselor for help with learning to connect with his peers and to get along better at work. He said the counselor told him to succumb to the small talk and humor the others. Bryant did not see this as a viable option for him because he tried it once and he was intolerant and frustrated. Bryant struggled with connection on all the 3 levels when we met.

Bryant expressed his frustrations, and he was open to avenues for solution. Bryant decided he would start with becoming more connected to his inner world in addition to his intellectual world. He said he could imagine success in this area. Bryant started to take Bikram Yoga because it was efficient, giving him results on all levels in a short time. Yes, he used this intellectual intensity to calculate the cost/benefit ratios quickly!

Months of yoga and Bryant was becoming more personable and aware of his inner landscape. He could share what made him angry, sad, happy, and even joyful. Bryant said he was feeling more alive and aware on other levels. Next, Bryant worked on his connection with his peers. He attempted to engage in conversation that was more social. He studied the local news and even watched a few TV shows he heard his peers talking about in the break room. He found that taking these small steps changed how his workday turned out each day. He told me that he actually went home with more energy and happier than ever before. He simply connected more fully with himself and then was more willing to extend himself in relationship to others. His career skyrocketed.

Bryant called after receiving a substantial promotion. He was told that he wasn't receiving the promotion earlier because of his lack of social awareness within the treatment team. He said he did not know this and was grateful that he chose to seek my counsel and make changes that made him feel more confident.

There is great power in connection. Our neurology and biology require connection to others of the same species. We are mammals with some extra special sensitivities and intensities. As with Bryant, improving authentic connection in one area yields opportunity for enhanced connection in other areas. Connection to self and being willing to look within and uncover unconscious beliefs and habits is essential to your life.

Honoring connection rather than perpetuating separation is needed in our world these days. The insensitivities that you run into on a daily basis can be efficiently navigated using your deep inner connection to your sensitivities and inner guidance. This is one powerful area where you can use your intense sensitivities in your favor as you live your vision.

Points to Ponder:

1. What are the ways you connect with nature and the universe at large?

2. How do you connect with others? Humans? Animals? Plants?

3. Do you invest in developing your inner connection?

4. Do any of your intense sensitivities block or slow your ability to connect?

5. How do you use your connections in service of others?

CHAPTER X.

Release Fear, Procrastination, and Perfectionism

Perfectionism is the willingness to be imperfect.

~~ Lao Tzu

Fear, procrastination, and perfectionism can be vexations to the soul. Fear does, however, get a bad rap. I have found that to be free of the seeming gripping impact of fear, I focus more on its function than its perceived power. The function of fear is to get ready. That's it. Get ready. When my intense sensitivities begin to take on a mind of their own and fear or anxiety are trying to build, I take 3 long slow breaths and ask myself "What do I need to be ready for today?" Because our brains answer every question that is asked, I receive the answer. Nearly every time, the answer is not something fear producing in my rational mind, yet my intensities experience it so deeply that my experience can become skewed.

Fear's Function

Fear's function is to prepare you for what you need to do next. Fear of a snake prepares you to take the right action for your safety, be it running or standing still. It is fear that is helping you. We live in a culture that has villainized fear. Yes, I too have struggles with fear and the intensity and quickness it can seem to take over. This is not a reason to beat yourself up by looking at the power you have given fear historically. Today, you are free to begin a new history of using fear for its function rather than using it to scare yourself even further. No need to perpetuate inner danger responses and fatigue your adrenal glands.

Procrastination

Procrastination can stem from unbridled and undisciplined fear, and it can also stem from a deep belief that maybe you are not as worthy as others may think so self-sabotage or avoidance become your actions. Procrastination can be like a cancer that spreads to all areas of your life. This definitely holds you back.

When I run into procrastination in my actions, I consciously slow down and take some time to look at the procrastination and identify the message and meaning in the behavior. I listen to my self-talk. I determine what beliefs are unpinning the procrastination. I then identify healthy new actions to assist moving through the block using my intense sensitivities as the guiding force.

Perfectionism

Perfectionism can be a double-edged sword. It can help you hold a high standard of performance and integrity, and it can be a hindrance to your happiness and success by impeding your progress.

I have asked potential job applicants if they consider themselves to be a perfectionist. When they say yes and elaborate on this great trait, I often do not hire them. Why? Perfectionism is rooted with fear at its core. It is rigid and often static ridden. This does not serve many relationships well. I believe that a person who is open and teachable can be taught skills using their personal talents which is much more aligned for me than running up against perfectionism and agendas that are promoted by fear and a sense of having to make up for secretly thinking you are not measuring up or a fraud somehow.

As an intensely sensitive person, you may want to release your attachment to fear and perfectionism. A better use of fear is to use it to help you prepare for what you must be doing or taking care of today. You can use the sense of perfectionism to be a trigger for you when you are becoming rigid, and many want to breathe and look at the situation from another vantage point.

Releasing attachment does not mean you will never feel fear again. It means that some of these beliefs and old patterns no longer have a hold on you because you are not attached to them. Non-attachment is about being fully engaged while releasing attachment to the outcome while detachment means being disconnected to the activity in a non-caring or resentful manner.

To release fear, perfectionism and procrastination is to take away the power these experiences have over you. By shifting the way you engage and interact with these 3 amigos, you regain your authority. You are in charge of your life, and you have the authority. Yes, these things can be challenging. This is where support, knowledge and shifting your mindset is useful. You will experience more freedom as you release your attachment to fear and perfectionism. Begin to focus on self-love and self-compassion as a solid start.

Over Reactivity

Being overreactive is a common trait of sensitive and intense people. Do you overreact at times? You most likely have allowed your egoic self to help protect your sensitive and vulnerable nature from the insensitive world. Initially, I imagine it was the best choice whether you were aware of it or not. You may even have an inner critic or inner judgmental voice that perpetuates fear. When your fear level is high, you tend to overreact in different ways. Some overreact by verbally yelling or shutting down or crying. Some simply freeze and procrastinate making any decision or taking any action.

Over-reactivity can be external where everyone can see your intensities and the out loud expression of them. It can also be internal when you take the excess vulnerable energy out on yourself with toxic self-talk or even self-deprecating thoughts. Severe depression or catatonia is a form of some type or over reaction, even if the person is not aware of it at the time.

Take a minute and look at your reactions to everyday living. Are you overreacting to life circumstances or challenges? Do you ever say to yourself, "Where is my overreacting behavior impacting?" when referring to the intensity of your emotions or intensity of your response. Have you ever opened your mouth and what came out was far more intense and penetrating than you imagined? All these are examples of being overreactive.

When you are tired or weary, you may be more overreactive. If your fear levels are elevated (especially existential fears) you may be more overreactive. If you are procrastinating and your inner voice is screaming at you, you may be overreactive. When you are judging or holding contempt or resentment, you may be a candidate for over-reacting. Add to this an emotional and/or intellectual overexcitability and you could be experiencing the perfect storm.

The antidote to overreacting comes in several steps or actions:

- Stop for a few minutes and breathe.

- Remind yourself that everything is OK and that there are no emergencies, not really. If there are, then call 911.

- After a couple minutes of quiet breathing, ask yourself, "Am I experiencing any fear in the moment"?

   ○ Fears can include being afraid of not getting what you want, being afraid of losing what you have, fear of your own vulnerability, and fear regarding your survival.

- It may be useful to call a supportive person from your peer groups or your mentor, therapist, or coach. Being unconditionally listened to can most often soothe the over reactivity and make your next steps easier. As a mentor for sensitive intense people, I am available to listen and support; asking effective questions whenever any of my clients or colleagues are dealing with fears or over reactivity.

- Be honest with yourself and now quietly evaluate ONE next right action to take that can help you regain your focus.

- Take the action. Breathe and allow the relief to wash over you.

- Take the next action, breathing and using supportive self-talk.

Now is the time to allow those who are supportive of you to listen to you, so you can discharge the energy. Then the solutions and actions become clear. Most often, the listening ear of a like-minded person can offer the clarity you are seeking yet cannot connect with because of the intense emotions and fears. Often the listener simply listens because your solutions are typically evident as you speak. Hearing yourself can offer many viable solutions and effective next actions. There is great power in supportive others who are willing to listen and hold your confidence.

As your storm quiets, take some time to relax and nurture your inner intense self. Stretch, drink some water then move on with your day. Remind yourself that being overreactive in a destructive or self-deprecating way is fear based. In those times you are allowing your sensitivities to turn on you. Therefore, having support people and a strategy to regain inner clarity is so vital. Your intensities are here to serve you and when they seem like a curse, you have the power to reorient them toward your authentic vision. Sometimes it takes some time and can be easier said than done. Thus, the value in connections.

Over Responsibility

Over responsibility is another gifted trait that can be heightened by overexcitabilities. Being hyper-responsible can add stress and fear to your life which then can cause all kinds of upsets and challenges. You are responsible for you and you alone. The moment you begin a sentence of responsibility with another person's name, you are treading into risky territory. Blame is dangerous.

Holding expectations of others that can impact your sense of well-being is also dangerous. When you expect someone else to do or be something, you are setting yourself up for disappointment. It may not happen and often it doesn't; yet the expectation alone adds vulnerability to your already intense way of living. If you are pointing a finger at another, there are 3 fingers pointing back at you.

You are not responsible for others and their actions. In business, having clear directions and criteria for success makes making decisions easier. Allowing your written directions to assist in achieving outcomes helps keep your emotional intensity within manageable levels so you end up not regretting anything you might say or do.

You are responsible for you. What is on your side of the street? Everything else is on another's side of the street. Resist your fear-based seeming need to take on more responsibility than is yours.

When you recover your vitality and can live authentically, you are free of the fears that were binding you. You will feel despair and the silent pain fall away and you will feel more alive, even younger.

Meet Rob

Rob is a successful entrepreneur who enjoys creating solutions for his community of followers and clients. Rob is creative and he enjoys being a specialist in some areas. He also has great intuitive skills that he speaks about rarely. I have seen his skills at work on the water, being tactically excellent in yacht racing. He uses his sensitivities and his intensities in his work and play!

Rob struggles with perfectionism at times and can overreact in tense situations. He states that he "feels my intensity colliding with my sensitivities and I sometimes act and speak out of character." Rob has a great sense of humor and those of us to know him love and appreciate his quirky ways.

Rob ran into some added challenges when he was encouraged by his business advisor to write a book and create more written content. Rob is great with verbal language, but he never saw himself as an author. He asked me about writing books as I had a few published at the time. We spoke and he reluctantly began to follow his advisor's advice to create written content.

A few weeks into his book writing, I received a call from Rob. He was frustrated, angry and on the verge of tears stating he was going to stop and give up on the book. He was finally excited about the topic, but he was not able to find a comfortable groove of writing, so he was giving up. After he talked until he was completely finished speaking. I listened to everything he said, and I also listened to everything he did not say. I asked a few questions. We talked and identified his obstacles. He identified fear, perfectionism and feeling overly responsible for the outcome and response by others. He was afraid of his brand being diluted, of what others would think, of his own vulnerability, of his perfectionism and more.

Rob was gripped by some very real challenges that are common with intensely sensitive people. He was feeling intensely, thinking deeply, and feeling compelled to produce at a high level. This was a perfect storm for Rob that we worked through. He had to go within a safe place to determine if the book was really for him to write or was there another way to share his ideas and genius. Just because someone told him it was a great idea, does not mean it was for him to complete.

Rob had to work through his desire to please others and focus on following his inner calling. I shared with Rob the idea that his challenge was not about what he could do (he could do anything he puts his mind to), rather it was about staying in integrity about what he is called to do. Aligning intellect, heart and soul are vital for maintaining inner integrity for intensely sensitive people. Rob was having sleepless nights, stomach issues and muscle tension and soreness.

Rob eventually decided to put the book on hold until further notice, giving himself permission to follow his inner wisdom and guidance. His advisor was confused and yet Rob held his ground. Rob told me that he felt free because he was no longer pressuring himself to follow the masses when he knew deep within that writing a book was not for him to do at this time. Rob did discern that a YouTube channel and video was much more his style. He launched the channel, is having fun and serving his audience.

The moment Rob focused on his inner alignment and integrity, possibilities and opportunities opened, and he was able to find a groove that was fulfilling and rewarding. He also noticed that this inner flow helped his yacht racing. By trusting his own inner guidance, Rob won more races by following great tactics that he could "see". I am thrilled for Rob. He is an intensely sensitive person with great gifts. As he has learned to acknowledge and trust his gifts, he is flourishing.

Points to Ponder:

1. In what ways do you experience fear?

2. In what ways do you procrastinate?

3. Are you a perfectionist? If so, how has it served you?

4. Does fear stop you from starting your projects that support your vision?

5. How does your attachment to perfectionism serve and hinder you?

CHAPTER XI.

Release Blocks to Thrive

Surviving is important. Thriving is elegant.

~~ *Maya Angelou*

Releasing Blocks

Everyone has blocks. You have blocks, I have blocks. We all have blocks. The important thing for intensely sensitive people is to release the static energy of the blocks so you can move forward. Because of feeling and experiencing life so intensely, you may struggle with releasing any block or challenge that frustrates you. How kind and compassionate are you with you?

It is important to create safety in your thought life. Having safety in your consciousness means there are no landmines waiting to blow you up without notice. The first and more important step is to become aware of your self-abusive inner dialogue and become willing to make some changes.

Kindness toward your inner self is vital when it comes to releasing old blocks. Remember that some of the blocks were unconscious and not immediately known to you in words yet you still feel it and experience its impact in your world. Kindness is the answer. Kindness melts away those pesky blocks. Anger and frustration reinforce the block.

Trying to push away or fight your blocks does not yield productive results. Whatever you fight or resist gets larger. Always remember that where your attention goes, your energy flows. If you focus on fighting a particular block, then that block will become more daunting because of you focusing on it . Rather, focus on solutions and being kind to yourself, knowing that the solutions of how to dissolve the block comes easily and effortlessly for you. Using your imagination and ability to shift your mind is very important. You get what you are focusing on and giving emotional energy to.

Meet Melissa

When I met Melissa, she bragged about being hard on herself and demanding perfection. She wore this as a badge of honor. She was frustrated that there were so many challenges, problems, and obstacles in her life. She was so focused on these that our first hour together was a nearly non-stop litany of problems and "I cant's." Any attempt I made to interject or ask questions was met with an even more intense description of the wrongs in Melissa's life. When she finally wound down, I asked if there was anything else. She said no.

Melissa had addictions. She was addicted to the familiar pain of being the victim, the pleasure of talking, and to her identifiers of being too intense, too sensitive, introverted, alone and female. She did not see this coming. These addictions were in her blind spot. She pushed back at me saying that she did not do drugs.

As we talked and I explained the patterns that become addictive and ingrained in her neurology, she could see the addictive nature of her functioning in the world. You can be just as addicted to neurochemicals traveling in a certain pattern as you can to some outside substance. Once the trigger happened, Melissa was off and running, she could not have stopped herself.

I define addiction as "you can't get enough of what you don't want." This includes problems, blockages, obstacles, fear, and the like. Melissa was miserable yet she was unable to stop herself from the debilitating pattern.

For many intensely sensitive folks, shutting down and hiding behind a fabricated veil/mask is a choice they have made. If you are one of those who is playing small or acting average to get along, it is time to come out from behind the mask and be your true self. You have great value. Your talents, gifts and sensitivities are needed now. You do not have your constellation of qualities and talents by accident. You deciding to use your intensities for the benefit of all concerned will certainly fulfill your vision.

Surviving to Thriving

Your purpose and your vision are meant to serve in some manner. They work together in tandem as a type of elegance in the Universe and your unique role. When you have been numbing yourself, or playing small, you have been in survival mode. There is nothing wrong with being in survival mode. Survival mode can become boring and stifling, causing low energy and lack of motivation. A more fulfilling and satisfied life comes from thriving in who you are and what you bring forth from within.

Your vision is personal to you and only you can bring it forth. No outside force can do it for you. This is a great joy and a great challenge. By saying yes to both the joy and the challenge, you set yourself up for a thriving life, full of richness and depth.

Looking for outside validation of your vision can distract you from realizing your heart's desire. Your vision is uniquely yours. Sometimes well-meaning people can be fearful and deter your authentic realization of your dreams. Remember that your vision is between you and the Divine. It was not a conference call so no one else has the exact same vision, mission, intensities, and sensitivities that come together in perfect order for your personal mission.

Your Joy is in living from the inside out while knowing inherently that Joy is your natural, authentic state. The challenge is remembering this when distractions or outdated beliefs creep in as they do for everyone. You can be Joy and have other feelings as well at the same time. They are not mutually exclusive.

When Joy is how you describe your state, you are truly thriving.

Meet Marie

Marie was a young adult when we first met. She had been struggling with substance abuse and was labeled difficult by her college professors. She was trying to function her best in school. When we met, she was on multiple psychiatric medications and her family was being told that she has severe problems.

Marie and I developed a rapport very rapidly. I could see her inner suffering while trying to please everyone else. She was bright and had a quick wit. As she remained abstinent from illicit substances, she began to clear up mentally and was more active physically. She eventually began to complain about feeling sedated from her medications. We located a local psychiatrist who was well versed in the intensely sensitive and gifted worlds. Upon the recommendation of the psychiatrist, Marie began to lower some medications slowly. Marie continued her recovery and work with me as she adjusted. Some days were more difficult than others as Marie was changing a pattern that was several years old.

Eventually, Marie was able to remain abstinent and off all medication. She states she was happy she moved slowly and worked on her emotion management as she progressed. Marie is a talented artist, and she is a great creative genius. She has a spiritual intensity that shines forth through her empathy and intuition.

Points to Ponder:

1. What blocks are you aware of in your way of your thriving?

2. What makes up the blocks?

3. In what life areas are you most blocked?

4. In what life areas are you thriving?

5. What does the bridge look like that carries you toward enhanced thriving?

6. How can kindness toward yourself assist you?

Chapter XII.

The Importance of Compassion

Compassion is sometimes the fatal capacity for feeling what it is like to live inside somebody else's skin. It is the knowledge that there can never really be any peace and joy for me until there is peace and joy finally for you too.

~~ Fredrick Buechner

COMPASSION

Compassion toward yourself brings about great results. Highly sensitive people tend to be hard on themselves. I'll bet you are no exception. You probably are also a time optimist which creates additional stress and challenges at times. Compassion is the way of being that offers humble kindness for the great adventure of being human with all its blunders and greatness.

Having compassion for yourself rather than beating yourself up constantly is a great way to begin to achieve the goals you deserve.

Compassion can be defined as positive thoughts and feelings that foster the rise of hope, courage, determination, and inner strength. In the Buddhist tradition, compassion is the wish for another being to be free from suffering. Compassion has many operational definitions as well as a myriad of expressions.

Compassion is the root of forgiveness. The first order of action regarding compassion is looking within yourself and freely offering compassion to yourself for all the blunders, follies, and mistakes of being human. Yes, life is a rich amazing journey. Intense sensitives tend to be overly self-critical or self-denying. Both are a result of being intensely sensitive in an insensitive world. Compassion for self, for the grand adventure of being human is the cornerstone for your peace of mind and fulfillment. Sometimes this can seem impossible or elusive, I promise self-compassion is attainable.

Compassion for others and their journeys is also important. This does not mean you compromise yourself or put yourself in harm's way. You can have compassion from a distance and not humanly enter the lion's den knowingly. Compassion is a way of being, it is not a thing you have that you get to give away so you can feel better about yourself. Compassion is a way – not an event as many are fooled into believing.

Being internally gentle is a hallmark sign of a compassionate person. Are you gentle with your inner self? This does not mean being weak or a doormat. You can be gentle with firm boundaries when you know who you are and the principles by which you are living.

Be sure to always live by your higher principles. When you stray, return as soon as possible. This is not about perfectionism; it is about living authentically from the inside out. Intense sensitives respond deeply to everyday, ordinary life. This is a great gift. Cherish the richness and depth of your being.

Compassion is a vital part of your survival as a human being. When selfishness begins to surface, compassion may appear to be taking a back seat. In these times of awareness, take a few breaths and focus on your self-compassion and allow this to extend to others. This will help ease the tension of the egoic selfishness that can undermine your serenity and harmony.

The Meaning of Compassion

The meaning of compassion is to recognize the suffering of others and then take action to help. Compassion embodies a tangible expression of love for those who are suffering.

The spirit of the word compassion is synonymous with doing. Compassion is not concerned with material or physical things. It's concerned with the human spirit and soul. The spiritual definition of compassion involves acting to alleviate the suffering of others.

Empathy vs. Compassion

Many may think that empathy and compassion are the same, yet they are quite different. Empathy is an ability to relate to another person's pain as if it's your own. Empathy is grounded in your emotion and feeling. Empathy does not have an active component like compassion demonstrates.

Empath Distress Disorder

Many empaths I have worked with also have some physical health challenges caused from the distress of absorbing others' energy and emotions. I call this Empath Distress Disorder. Empaths are pro-foundly energy sensitive and often the energy is absorbed by them without them really knowing until they feel "off" somehow.

One client has sleep problems and has dreams that are ex-emplary of the energy he has been around while another client experiences digestion and hunger irregularities when she is taking on energies that are not her own. I know a couple people who are in the helping professions that have experienced serious sickness as a result of taking on so much energy from others that it made their own body toxic.

By doing the deeper spiritual work, they have rectified their challenges and are now healthier. The key is making friends with your empathic self and your intense sensitivities and using healthy bound-aries to keep your world and body free of energetic intrusions.

Compassion Fatigue

Compassion without clear, healthy boundaries can lead to compassion fatigue. Compassion fatigue is a condition characterized by emotional and physical exhaustion leading to a diminished ability to empathize or feel compassion for others, often described as the negative cost of caring. It is sometimes referred to as secondary traumatic stress.

Compassion fatigue is characterized by utter emotional, mental, and physical exhaustion. It ushers in a diminished ability to empathize or feel compassion for others or oneself. In the helping professions, this is often described as the negative cost of caring too much with squishy boundaries. I have experienced this when I was beginning my career and on occasion in my early years. The culprit in my case was that I found myself caring more for the welfare of the client than the client cared for themselves. This can be a common way to fatigue yourself. The very quality that makes you great at your craft can also cause significant trouble if not recognized properly.

If you are naturally intense and empathic and you begin to notice your connection becoming clouded or disconnected. Compassion fatigue could be speaking to you through your detachment and burnout. After becoming detached you may become irritable or chronically frustrated in situations where your irritability does not match the current situation. An example is being very irritated and frustrated that someone is taking too long to finish their sentence or even being angry that others may be smiling. This disconnection erodes your sense of connection to your essence.

Compassion fatigue has also been called secondary traumatic stress. In other words, the helper is taking on the traumatic stress of the helpee and the fatigue that ensues also has a traumatic response in the helper. This is not noble. I remember learning that it was noble to have compassion fatigue because it means you care. Yes, care – AND care with boundaries that protect your well-being.

Many people seek help for stress related health concerns because of compassion fatigue. This can come about through work when you are in a helping profession or from world or family events when you deeply care. Holding the space for compassion while not tending to your needs is the recipe for a deep fatigue that can be debilitating. It is not noble to give to the point of self-harm.

If left unaddressed, compassion fatigue can progress into serious life consequences. Paying attention to the warning signs and honoring your inner experience makes a great difference while affording you a way to stop the fatigue and regain your sense of joy and well-being.

My current practice is to give no more to the relationship and outcome than my client is giving. My inner boundary allows for growth, expansion while I retain my vital energy.

The Importance of Compassion

The value of compassion enables you to understand yourself better and others better. With understanding our inherent desire to relieve suffering is allowed to emerge in a healthy way. It is important for intense sensitives to cherish the ability to deeply connect with others and to develop the capacity to experience their world as we offer support, encouragement, and empathy.

Empathy and compassion for the grand adventure of being human with all its ups and downs is a vital part of being intensely sensitive.

Points to Ponder:

1. What is compassion?

2. How do you experience empathy?

3. Have you ever experienced compassion fatigue?

4. How does compassion emerge in your thoughts, words, and actions?

5. Do you offer compassion to yourself and others?

Chapter XIII.

Healthy Boundaries

Boundaries are your responsibility. You decide what is and isn't allowed in your life.

~~ Brittney Moses

Boundaries for smart and sensitive folks could be an entire book! Boundaries are important, both in relation to others and in relation to yourself. Your boundaries are vital to your health in all areas of your life. There are 2 general areas of boundaries to consider. Both are equally important.

There are the boundaries that are externally focused. These are the criteria you use to determine how close someone gets to you, whether it be mentally, physically, emotionally, or spiritually. Some level of permission to be in each other's space is so very important. Crossing someone's boundaries, even inadvertently for a good reason, can cause a disruption for them and you.

Then there are your inner boundaries. Many people do not focus here yet I believe these to be especially important. Your inner boundaries help you decide how much of you that you bring to the situation or event. Smart and intensely sensitive people are greatly impacted by these boundaries due to the inner intensities going on that others cannot see. It is critical that you give yourself permission to regulate how much of you comes out in any situation. This is a way to maintain integrity by being your authentic self in concert with the circumstance at hand. For example: I bring different facets of myself forward when I am racing a sailboat than when I am teaching a class on spiritual principles in daily living. Both are authentically me emerging with discernment.

There are distinct types of boundaries that apply to both internal and external boundaries. Here are a few examples as they relate to gifted, intense, sensitive folks.

Types of Boundaries:

Mental/Intellectual Boundaries – These boundaries have to do with your thinking, beliefs, and intellectual pursuits. What you allow into your world is important. You cannot undo what you see or hear. This includes ideas, conversations, and all thinking intellectually or mental in nature.

Emotional Boundaries – Emotional boundaries include what emotions you allow in your presence and by whom for how long. They are how close you allow someone get to you on an emotional level. Some people do not watch violent entertainment because their emotions do not vibe with the chaos and destruction. Some people dislike drama because of the emotions that are evoked.

Physical/Material Boundaries – Physical and material boundaries are about your physical being and your stuff. What permission you give others to be in proximity to you. This includes your material possessions. These are the most common things when people talk about boundaries. This is one aspect and certainly all the others are equally important.

Temporal Boundaries – Time boundaries are about timeliness and respecting self and others by respecting time. Chronic lateness is an issue with temporal boundaries. The person who is chronically late is equally responsible as the person who tolerates the lateness and harbors silent upset or frustration.

Social Boundaries – Social boundaries are about what is okay and not okay socially. This includes dress, language, conversation content, etiquette and more. Gifted people often struggle with social boundaries and may be served with support in this area. Learning some social ques and ways to engage based on the audience is vital to social confidence.

Sexual Boundaries -Sexual boundaries have to do with how you express yourself as a sexual being. Using your sexuality to bully or control another as well as using your sexuality to play victim are all questionable boundaries. What you will allow in your presence is part of your sexual boundary structure.

Spiritual Boundaries – Spirituality is about being connected to the greater universal life force. We can all feel the energy of others as we approach each other. This is spiritual energy. How do you establish your healthy boundaries regarding what you allow in your life? Empaths must pay close attention as you may be picking up on energy that is not yours and may not be local to you, yet it is very real. You have belief systems around spirituality, and these are boundaries that are important to discern effectiveness, usefulness, and clarity.

Inner Boundaries – Your inner boundaries refer to how much of you is being brought to any situation or engagement. Intense and sensitive people are often told they are too much or too sensitive. You are the one in charge of how much of you that you bring to any situation. You will bring different amounts of your intense sensitivities to the store than you will in intimate relationships. By learning to align how much of you comes forth in a given situation, you conserve your energy while also being well received.

Setting Healthy Boundaries Requires:

1. **Attunement/Tuning in** – the more you gain connection to your inner landscape, the more effective your boundaries will be. Tuning in to your inner energy as well as tuning into what is happening in the outer, helps you discern your next best actions. Learning to tune in is vital. Attunement allows you flexibility and freedom in how to show up and respond to any given situation. Pay attention to your inner knowing and learn to trust this knowing as a valuable resource.

2. **Willingness** – This is often overlooked. Being hardheaded or stubborn can work against healthy boundaries. You want to develop an inner willingness to experience life in safe and healthy ways. This requires inner honesty and an open-minded posture toward life. Be willing to investigate your inner world.

Be willing to be curious about the world at large. Be willing to say "No" when necessary. Be willing to take a stand for your authentic self. Willingness goes a long way in your mental and spiritual health.

3. **Speaking Up/Clear Communication** - Clear communication and speaking up are vital. Allowing confusion, mixed messages, and chaos to stop you from getting your needs met is a misuse of your boundary system. Using your voice may be challenging at times while navigating intense responses to your inner world or environment. Breathing deeply and calming your system will allow for more possibilities to emerge. There are many ways to speak up and having a mentor or guide may be helpful as you find your voice.

4. **Clearly Communicated Priorities** – You are sick in generalities and healthy in specifics. The clearer you are the better. When you are vague or overly general in your communication it allows room for misunderstanding and boundary violations, both conscious and unconscious. Do the people close to you know your priorities? Are you clear about your priorities and your needs? Being non-committal and general opens the door for problems in your relationships. The clearer and more precise you are with your thoughts, language, and actions, the happier you will be in your daily life.

5. **Flexibility** – Being flexible is a requirement. Being curious is part of being flexible. When you can bend and not break because of being rigid, you open doors to creating more effective boundaries that work. Like a cell membrane, you want to be open and receptive to some things while also being locked to other things. This flexibility makes you more pliable and therefore your flow is enhanced. "The only constant is change" as Socrates said. Being flexible affords you the opportunity to change your mind, to learn and grow and expand and to step back and withdraw when appropriate. This is all part of having a healthy, fluid boundary structure.

6. **Respect for the Boundaries of Others** – Part of a healthy boundary system is engaging with the boundaries of others with respect. When someone sets a boundary, listen to them and act in kind. When you respect others' boundaries you will also grow the respect level within the relationship. If the other is trying to trap you, you will be able to see this behavior quickly. If someone sets a boundary and you respect it and then they get upset or try to get you to go back and forth, then there is an undisclosed motive at hand. Your respect of their boundary and the undisclosed motive both show up simply by you being respectful.

Points to Ponder:

1. Define Boundaries.

2. How do you use your inner and outer boundaries?

3. What happens when someone pushes your boundaries?

4. How do you feel when you break your own boundaries?

5. What boundaries are serving you most currently?

6. What boundaries could use some enhancement or improve-ment in your life?

CHAPTER XIV.

Being Your Authentic Self

The authentic self is the soul made visible.

~~ *Sarah Ban Breathnach*

It is not what you say, it is how you say it. Authenticity is one of the most highly revered qualities these days. For intensely sensitive people, this can be a big risk. You may have had times when you were real and authentic, and you were misunderstood or somehow felt alienated from others. Strong sensitivities can be a challenge at times. Your intensities can also support and enhance your authenticity. There is immense power in human emotions and when you can live fully in your authenticity without shrinking around others, your inner light shines brightly, and your vision is alive!

Giving yourself permission to be authentic requires self-love and a sense of knowing who you are as a unique sensitive person. To live by the Higher Principles, means that you are kind and compassionate with yourself as well as true to who you are and what you bring to any situation or relationship.

Humanistic psychologists might say that authentic people possess common characteristics that show they are psychologically mature and fully functioning as human beings. These might include having realistic perceptions of reality, accepting of self and others, good sense of humor, able to express emotions clearly, and can learn from mistakes. I believe that there are more considerations in a practical manner when it involves complex, intense and sensitive people. There are many factors that can alter self-expression and levels of maturity.

The ways of defining authenticity in mainstream psychology may not be your experience. Your reality is much more diverse and intricate than any generalization can address. Simply take what works.

For me, being authentic means that you are your real self - coming from a place of inner integrity and alignment – mind, heart, gut, and soul. Here are some considerations of nuance for intensely sensitive people.

Introversion

Introversion means you are oriented toward your internal, private world of your inner thoughts and feelings. Introverts are more withdrawn, retiring, reserved, quiet, and deliberate; they tend to mute or guard expression of thoughts, ideas or facial expressions while adopting a more skeptical view of the situation. Many introverts prefer to work independently. Team projects were challenging for me in school. I am very introverted, and I can also be social and follow great ideas and inspiration.

Many gifted people are introverts at heart. Refueling alone. Introverts have a strong reaction to chaos or too much noise. Some of my introverted clients say they love to replenish their batteries alone rather than enjoy engaging with others.

As an introvert, you may be misjudged as aloof, angry, or distant because of your nature to listen and sit back initially. I know I have had to teach some people around me that my quiet is not dismissive, rather I am processing internally. This is a very different strategy from my extroverted counterparts.

Every introvert has a great inner resource. In our extroverted society, introversion sometimes gets a bad rap. This is an opportunity to use your unique intensities and sensitivity to your advantage.

Neurodiversity

Neurodiversity, in a practical sense, means that all humans vary in their neurocognitive ability. Everyone has unique gifts and talents, and everyone has unique struggles. For some intensely sensitive people this neurodiverse variation between strengths and perceived weaknesses can be profound. The road can be challenging and exciting at the same time. Having people who understand and honor your intensely sensitive nature is a requirement for healthy living.

Neurodiverse people experience, interact with, and interpret the world in unique and varied ways. It is time we address the cultural stigma around learning and thinking differences. Our egos want us to believe that we all think the same and in reality, we all process and think differently. There is great beauty in this understanding. No two people engage with the world the same.

You and I experience the world through our autobiography and our makeup. These come together to create our unique and very personal life experience. No two people do life the same. Neurodiverse/neurodivergent people find some parts of daily life easy and fun while other aspects can be very challenging. When your thoughts, words, and actions become inconsistent or irregular, check in with how you are processing the world. Your unique experience will help you with challenges as well as show you areas to enhance and excel.

You are an intensely sensitive person, so your experiences will have more variety, depth, undulations, and intensities than many of your family and peers. Every neurodiverse person is unique even though there are many similarities. Your neurodiversity can also be a competitive advantage when your strengths can emerge to the forefront. There is great value in open, diverse, and inclusive environments that allow for your intensities, sensitivities, and neurodiversity to shine.

Because you process differently and you have a deep, rich inner experience, you are also vulnerable to the temptation to try to fit in or hide your exceptionalities. This is counterproductive. Instead, access resources to assist to help align your world to meet your intense sensitivities in their sweet spot. As you make friends with you and you seek those who understand, and there are many of us, you will certainly notice more joy and flow entering your life from the inside out because of the permission to be you!

Intense Sensitivities and Giftedness Runs in Families

So many of the traits that indicate giftedness are common among extended family members. Parents may see a sign of giftedness and consider it perfectly normal, average behavior if several family members have the same trait. I remember when I was in my first days of college. I called my mother and said, "I get it now. What we call normal is divergent from the normal of others. No wonder things felt so different all along". This insight was a profound moment of self-acceptance and permission to be my quirky and eccentric self.

When you live around gifted, intense, and sensitive people you begin to normalize the experience. Others may ask you to dial it back or tone it down. There is no wrong way to be you. This is where inner boundaries are essential. Because of your unique constellation of neurodiverse processing, you can bring the needed facet to the forefront at will as you develop the skills. Now you have increased flexibility. This is where mentors and other support and encouragement is vital. The mirror of the other can show you avenues that were previously in your blind spot.

Meet the Smith Family

This family contacted me to work with the children in the family. The young people were struggling in school, and it seemed that their intense sensitivities were also impacting their relationship with their parents. The parents are gifted and were not yet aware of the deep meaning and nuance of being gifted and that every member of the family will have varied sensitivities and traits. Both parents are professional and dedicate themselves to their family. Though I was called to work with the children, the parents also required some attention as the mother was experiencing increasing anxiety while the father became more and more emotionally unavailable in the state of overwhelm from work and family responsibilities.

The children had an age range from 7 years old to 16 years old. The 7-year-old freely spoke about her intuition and connection to her deeper essence. Both parents were supportive of her expression and they had many questions for me. The other 3 siblings had varied amounts of overexcitabilities and spiritual sensitivities. As I got to know everyone, it became obvious that the intense sensitivities were prevalent in each member of the family.

As our work continued and each person, starting with the parents, learned about their giftedness and the relevance to their relationships and performance in work and school. With new understanding and awareness, there was an renewed sense of calm ad focus within the family system. From this place, we could delve deeper into rectifying and healing challenges and disruptions in their family system.

The oldest started to share that their aunt was similar to her and that they had great conversations. The parents did not know about this connection stating that they knew they loved each other yet did not know about the connection around spiritual sensitivities. As the parents began to look at their childhood and family life, they began to see gifted overexcitabilities and spiritual sensitivities in many relatives that showed up in varied ways.

Existential loneliness stems from the feeling that no one understands me really. As each person became more aware of the larger picture, they would share new conversations and awareness with me each time we met and in emails and texts as time has unfolded. Though there is some continued loneliness and angst at times, each person reports how helpful it is to see the world through the eyes as an intensely sensitive person with greater personal respect and sovereignty.

By each person being willing to learn about and accept the others' unique sensitivities, this family system was able to grow and develop together with increased harmony and understanding. We are still in contact and the parents report that by using their knowledge and understanding, "everyone is happier".

This Smith family is a melding of many of the families that I have worked with in various venues over the years. If you relate to any of this short story, I encourage you to explore how intense sensitivities run in your family system. This deeper understanding makes a profound difference in your relationships and understanding,

Points to Ponder:

1. How do you hide your authentic self?

2. When do you allow your authentic self to emerge without filters?

3. Describe your authentic self, including your intensities and eccentricities.

4. How is your family or a family you know similar to the Smith family?

Chapter XV.

Faith, Trust, and Imagination

Your imagination is your preview of life's coming attractions.

~~ Albert Einstein

For Intensely sensitive people, faith, trust, and imagination are cornerstones to many of the gifts and talents that others can identify. For many intense sensitives though, the talents seem obvious and can be taken for granted. For some, it is tempting to judge others using the same metric as oneself which can break rapport and create misunderstanding. We will explore each of these important facets. Pay attention to how these might apply uniquely in your life. You will experience them differently in accordance with your autobiography, sensitivities, intensities, and personal makeup. Honor your unique expression.

Faith

Faith is the substance of things hoped for and the evidence of things unseen as you read in Hebrews 11:1. It is also practically where you intersect with your belief system. Whatever you have faith in is where you place your energy of attention and intention. It is from this focus that your life comes into being. When you look around at your life, what do you see, feel, and experience? This reflects what you have had faith in over time. If there is anything that you do not desire, take the steps to change where you place your attention and faith.

Faith is often exhibited as gentleness, humility, and patience. As you develop increased connection to your inner faith, you will notice increased tolerance and a sense of inner gentleness that becomes obvious in your behaviors and voice tone. Your jaw will be more relaxed, and your body tension will reduce. As you allow your faith to emerge, your blood pressure will stabilize, and you will have better digestion because your body will be more relaxed and receptive.

Some faith is more conventional while other expressions of faith may be more intuitive. There is no wrong way. Belief and loyalty to what you say you have faith in are most powerful when aligned. Many gifted people who are trying to intellectualize their way through life may struggle here. At some point, you may want to focus on harmonizing your intellect, emotions, and faith as they all serve you in wonderful ways.

Meet Sean

Sean has a strong faith. We have worked together over the span of years in different capacities. Sean can quote various spiritual ideas and reports that his faith is strong. Yet Sean is plagued with ongoing struggles as an intense sensitive. Sean reports wanting to expand his awareness and understanding of faith, yet he continues to exhibit resistance to personal growth. Sean often deals with complacency that is accompanied by distraction and avoidance behaviors.

Having intellectual "faith" is very different than feeling into faith as a way of being. Sean tends to overthink and deny his emotional and spiritual connection to what he reports having faith in regarding work and relationships. This strategy has been ineffective for Sean. He becomes angry and easily frustrated when others do not adopt his views. When I have offered feedback, Sean will eventually slow down and say he wants to grow.

Sean has a history of distracting from his purpose by focusing on relationships and then ignoring his friends and family. Sean also has a history of irritability, judgment, and anger episodes in his work environment. He has repeatedly shared that "this is how I am" to excuse his behavior and harsh words. Sean asks for help then often ghosts those whom he contacts for assistance. Blame and lack of personal accountability have also plagued Sean, ending up in legal situations that he states he "should know better."

In our work, Sean has struggled with inner honesty and maintaining integrity in word and action. His giftedness and faith have been used by him as a way to be guarded from taking personal responsibility in some areas. These challenges for intense sensitives are formidable and often require strong support and direction.

Trust

Trust is an interesting topic. Many people view trust as only a positive and desirable quality and they use this as the litmus paper for whether there is trust or not in a person, group, or situation. I use the word trust a bit differently though I do not disagree with the popular and practical uses. As Paulo Coelho says, *"Trust your vibes; energy doesn't lie."*

Trust, for me, means consistency over time. If you are repeatedly 10 minutes late when we get together, then I trust that you will be 10 minutes late. When you make a change, then I will have to adjust. I may or may not like that you are 10 minutes late yet nevertheless I can trust this in your behavior. Consistency over time. Plato said that we get the behavior we tolerate, and he also said that we teach people how to treat us. These speak to trust within a relationship of any kind.

Trust is required for innovation, expansion, inspired ideas, collaboration, and productivity. Trust in self and trust in others can mean the difference between a powerful outcome and one that falls short. Trust allows for acceptance and support in your environment. Being dependable and building confidence invites you toward an expansive and reliable foundation whether it be a work or in a personal relationship.

Competency brings about confidence. As an intensely sensitive person, you also want to have self-compassion. Putting down the negative self-talk and learning to have inner integrity is important for your satisfaction and happiness. Look out for distractions and excuses that can invite you away from trusting yourself. These are the beginnings of adding more challenges to your life.

Meet Boyd

Boyd has an uncanny trust and connection with animals. An animal trainer by vocation, he communicates in ways that often amaze his co-workers and friends alike. Boyd once shared with me that he can tell what is happening with an animal much more accurately than a human. Boyd trusts the behaviors of animals where he says he cannot always trust humans. Humans can be consistently inconsistent which is challenging for sensitive people to deal with on a regular basis.

Trust is consistency over time and a relationship is built. Boyd struggles with the inconsistency in many humans who say one thing and do another. He told me that he can trust animals more because they give clear clues as to how they are doing and how their behavior aligns. Once you know the pattern, they are consistent. Boyd told me he likes this part of his work.

Boyd has a strong intuition that he refers to as his "gut". He can sense the animals and thus relies on the messages they send. He said this is easier than trying to decipher mixed human messages. Our work has largely been to help him make friends with his inherent gifts, talents, sensitivities and to find ways to use them in human interaction with more effectiveness.

Trust comes in behaviors as well as words. Boyd senses trust and sometimes because of his intensities, struggles with verbal evidence that he can trust. Boyd is using his connection and trust with animals as a powerful asset, and he works on accommodations for his verbal relationships where trust is valued in his family and with co-workers.

Imagination

Imagination is a very active part of your reality. Intensely sensitive people use imagination in overdrive! You already know that though. Whatever you can imagine, you can achieve when you apply faith, trust, and focused massive action. For some of you it is the focused, massive action part that can be elusive. After you imagine the great things, imagine you're taking focused action. It is in focused action that you will yield the most powerful results.

Your heightened association of impressions and images alongside your intuitive ability can yield powerful connections in various relationships of people and events. Your attention to precision and detail are great assets in your everyday life. I bet many people seek your opinion and vision for creative projects where the average needs to be elevated in ways they may not be able to initially identify.

Your complexity and nuanced thought process is evidenced by your sophisticated thinking style. You may also be able to integrate various pieces of information into a unified whole. Your imagination can take you down the path pf distraction as in daydreaming or dissociating. It can also foster meaningful connections of ideas and concepts.

Meet Veronica

Veronica's imagination has taken her on many adventures professionally and personally. As a natural artist and talent with space, color, and dimension, she uses her imagination to create the vision her clients describe to her in words. Veronica can see things others cannot when it comes to creativity and imagination.

At work, Veronica is the go-to person for new ideas and her visionary mindset. Veronica told me that she does not understand why others cannot see what she can see. She sees herself as average and others as either lazy or uninspired. As we worked together, Veronica began to see her sensitivity as a gift and her imagination as one of the many ways her intrinsic intense sensitivity is expressed.

Today, Veronica is able to accept compliments related to her imagination. She is learning to honor her intensities and sensitivities. Veronica shared recently that she is happier since embracing her inner wiring. Initially, Veronica confided in me that she did not trust her imagination and saw it more as a liability than an asset. As we are working together, Veronica is building self-confidence. I keep saying that great things are happening!

Many intensely sensitive and smart people often give themselves credit for accomplishing something when they thought about it yet never took any action. Then they wonder why things aren't turning out like they desire. Well, you must take action that focuses specifically on your vision. For example, If I want to publish this book, I must actually focus and put in the time and effort to do the work. Wishing it would be done and getting it done are not the same thing. For many intensely sensitive people, one time is a habit so having to take regular consistent action over time can be challenging. This is where having people in your life who you trust to be available to inquire about your progress and hold you accountable is a great asset.

Intensely sensitive people tend to be controlling and want things their way. This can lead to being closed-minded. When someone who is smart and sensitive tries to make a change in life, support, encouragement, and feedback loops are vital for success. If you try to go about any change in secret or alone, without others in your corner, you are making things very hard on yourself. The belief you have that you can do anything you put your mind to is true. You wouldn't have the idea if you could not achieve it someway, somehow. The key here is to realize that action with focus and determination are also necessary.

Delayed gratification is one of the hallmark traits of successful people. Delaying gratification may be a challenge for you when your intensities are running high. This helps you learn to manage your needs and is part of being emotionally intelligent. Delayed gratification is about delaying the impulse for immediate reward. In many areas of life, delaying gratification can be a powerful asset that yields success. This is another area to work with within yourself.

Points to Ponder:

1. Define Faith.

2. What is trust?

3. What role does your imagination play in your happiness?

4. How do you know you can trust yourself or another?

5. Do seeming lack of faith, trust or imagination cause you stress?

6. What does thriving look like to you? Is it attainable?

CHAPTER XVI.

Leaving Your Legacy

Please think about your legacy because you're writing it every day.

~~ *Gary Vaynerchuck*

One of the most effective ways to leave your legacy is to teach what you know to others, especially to those who are coming behind you. You have many life lessons and many experiences that are of great value. Take a minute now and reflect on a few of your many lessons that you are willing to pass on. Maybe you will write them down for others or maybe do a video. Will you be posting on social media or sharing in a business setting or at a family gathering? Being willing to freely share your journey and the lessons that you have gleaned is vital to living your vision as an intense person.

Your inherent gifts and intensities coupled with being sensitive on many levels makes you uniquely qualified to offer wisdom that many will not develop without your teaching, guidance, and willingness to share. What comes naturally to you is not always natural for others. In fact, your personal gifts and sensitivities are not experienced the same as any other person. This is one of the amazing aspects of having multiple peer groups. It is the coming together that the real magic of life happens!

In my decades of working with bright and gifted, often intensely sensitive people enjoy exploring their multi-potential and intense worlds. Common intense sensitivities include profound inner spiritual guidance, intellectual prowess, deep and abiding empathy and a strong inherent sense of justice. These are some of the amazing powerful and intense gifts that come with being an intensely sensitive person trying to make it in an insensitive world. I have had the honor of being witness to profound and transcendent experiences while holding the sacred space for the expression of each person's genius.

The work here is integrating on a higher level, these experiences with daily life. With many of my clients, I am the voice to remind them of taking the time and opportunity to integrate. Choosing to examine and follow the higher calling of pursuing an existential understanding of life takes focus, passion, and tenacity. When the world wants you to dumb down yet your inner being is pulsing so strongly that to stop the emergence would be painful, what do you do? I say that you honor your intense and profound experience, let the beauty and mess emerge into the world and allow the Universal power to assist in the experience and integration of the higher realms.

Your spiritual quest is the key component in your life, even when it does not follow along traditional lines. Your meaningful experiences and connections may be with nature, plants, sentient beings, The Divine or something more traditional. This spirituality diverges from traditional religion so many of my clients are receptive to being given permission to explore the higher realms in the way that serves their inner calling and vision. The message is about connection and allowing your inner impulse to come forth and be expressed. Once you allow this experience, you experience a powerful sense of flow and ease in life. You will have a "knowing" of your path and opening the doors and acting along that path will be effortless and open doors of awareness, understanding, and passion you didn't know were inside you.

When you have permission to breathe into the moments of connection, you thrive. Your life is forever changed for the better. You become free from the inside out. The undeniable, powerful, and inspiring connection may be short spurts or lasting connection times. Everyone has a different experience. Your experience is unique and sacred. Within these experiences are the seeds of your legacy. Plant the seeds and allow them to germinate and grow. You will look back with awe on your journey. It will unfold in ways you never imagined. You are eternally altered. Intense sensitivity, positive disintegration and the unforgettable spiritual experiences will certainly mold and shape your future.

Some people do not seek or wish to explore their higher connection. Some believe there is a connection and seeking is not interesting to them and some do not believe there is a connection to be experienced. There seems to be a difference in the seekers I work with and those who are not interested in seeking. Some are not seeking spiritual connection, yet they experience this connection unexpectedly and they are transformed! I wonder if it is necessary to be a spiritual seeker and grow along spiritual lines to live your legacy.

What is Spirituality?

This is a big question. There have been volumes upon volumes written about spirituality over the ages. Things I read go from very conservative proclamations to very esoteric interpretations. In all my theological studies, formal and informal, I have come to deeply appreciate the many paths available to you for your personal transformation. Even when you are not aware of it, you are moving along an amazing path on which you have free will and co-create your experience.

Spirituality includes questions of mortality, philosophy, business culture, psychology, politics, ethics, leadership, education as much as it is about seeking a higher connection. In my experience, these other disciplines are also filled with seekers. For me, it is the seeking that makes your journey spiritual in nature. In the seeking is the beauty and brilliance of your legacy.

Incorporating mindfulness and meditation in business culture is becoming the new business model across America. This is the impact of seeking and the beginning of a more prevalent understanding of the power of the practice of allowing your vision to emerge from the inside out. Many of the businesses I have helped create a mindful practice, did so because of the bottom-line financial gain initially. Over time, the overall benefit became apparent. Less absenteeism, more quality production, improved team morale and less turnover led to better business and personal relationships. This is especially important because key visionaries were psychologically safe enough to share their ideas and the companies expanded in ways never before considered. Now, we are using gifts of intense sensitivity for the good rather than judging and attempting to squash the emerging answers.

By allowing and supporting spiritual development into the business world, everyone benefits. I am heart warmed by these cultural changes. I have been an outlier for years and have endured many criticisms for my strong belief in this way to do business. Finally, it seems there is some breathing space, and we all benefit from the increased awareness as people begin to wake up and listen to their inner calling. In the action of the seeker is the transcendent healing of the old wounds and pain that societies have been carrying for far too long.

Meet Douglas

Douglas was a gifted and talented man who had no idea about intensities or spiritual sensitivities when we met. He was struggling in his marriage and with finding his best work or vocation. Douglas reported experiencing depression, anxiety, and melancholy. He could verbalize appreciation and love for his great family, yet there was something missing. He was determined to feel connected to his loved ones and have a sense of his purpose in life.

In our work together, Douglas revealed that he had a spiritual gift as a young boy and was made fun of by others, so he stifled this gift. He did not call it a gift initially. He shared that he would have dreams of creative ideas and events that would happen in school and his neighborhood. When he noticed that his dreams were coming true, his mother and teachers labeled this his overactive imagination. They told him not to make up stories after the fact about things that were happening. Douglas got bullied by his older brother and others at school. Douglas turned inward and shut down during this time. He was 6 years old.

Now, a father himself, he explained that he did not want to send these kinds of messages to his children, and he was fearful that he already "ruined them." We processed these feelings and his desires moving forward. I began to introduce Douglas to the gifted reality including overexcitabilities and brain development. As he listened and researched on his own, Douglas began to have many epiphanies. He reported understanding his childhood, adolescence, and adult feelings of being misunderstood, shame and fear about not being like the others. As he grew in awareness and made friends with himself and stopped some of his negative self-talk. Douglas' veil of sadness began to lift with understanding.

One day, Douglas stopped by my office to see if I was free for a minute. I was and invited him in so we could talk briefly. He told me he had a dream about me the night before and he was excited to share and could not wait until our next meeting. He shared about seeing me on a dock with many alabaster vases neatly stacked behind me. He knew that there was a spiritual meaning. He was excited. He said he knew the vases contained wisdom and information and that they were for me and from my angels. He had goosebumps while talking and his voice even picked up pace. I heard him and was open to his interpretation of his dream. Douglas was so excited. He shared how grateful he was that I took the time to listen as he left saying, "We can talk about the meaning when we meet."

Douglas revealed his spiritual sensitivity. His spiritual gifts that were coming through in the safety of his newfound awareness of his giftedness. We spoke about his spiritual clairvoyance and how it interacted with his imaginational intensity as a boy. He could see the misunderstanding by the adults who had no reference point or language at that time. Our work continued as Douglas began to stand in his identity as an intensely sensitive man who is a master creator. The more he embraced his inner wiring, the more he thrived. The more he learned and embraced his intense sensitivity, the more he and his family thrived. Today, Douglas uses his intense sensitivities in his work, and he has language to validate his children. We are in touch, and he shares that his life is doing well, and he is grateful for learning that he is not sick, he is uniquely gifted.

In my experience, gifted and intensely sensitive people tend to stay away from sharing their spiritual experiences because they have either been judged or ridiculed or are afraid of it happening if they open their mouth. This squashing of a vital part of their inner self is the cause of many life challenges from depression to addiction to self-harm. Some of my clients have tiptoed around the topic until I opened the door and gave permission for them to share. Most often, the look of relief on their faces has been profound. Once the door was opened and they realized they were safe, their real transformation blossomed.

These gifts can be expressed through their emotional intensity of their relationships with others or the Divine. These spiritual gifts and awareness are not always experienced or talked about in the terms of traditional paradigms. The beauty with creating a safe place for exploration and validation is that the road to your transformation and transcendence lies on the road that it is unfolding. This road is your legacy in motion.

What gets in the way of this great unfoldment is fear. Fear of ridicule or being further ostracized from family or peers. There are also many fear-based beliefs about what it means to be spiritually gifted or to be intense and be a seeker. The fears are designed by your ego to keep the status quo. Your inner seeker trying to emerge is meant to expand the status quo into a more fluid and profound life experience. After all, the only real constant is change so trying to keep things the same or even worse, going back to a previous time, is not productive and causes great pain.

Being intensely sensitive offers you a great opportunity to follow your inner heart's desire and ask profound questions. The answers you receive will show you the way. Much like headlights on a car driving on a winding mountain road, it takes faith that there is a road ahead even when you cannot yet see the road. It is your journey that matters most.

One common thread throughout my work with intense and gifted people of all ages is the predisposition and the capacity to connect to the spiritual world through their emotional, intellectual, and spiritual intensities and sensitivities. No matter their age, it is in giving permission for the exploration that brings forth the greatest reward and spiritual integration. Sometimes I simply listen, validate, ask questions of inquiry, and remind you that "It is all going to be okay, you are safe."

A trait of many of my clients has been a level of empathy and a sense of fairness or justice. Some of my people start out being resentful because things aren't fair, and they then begin their transformation. When you hold onto your resentment, you create suffering for you and those you love. Becoming open-minded and willing to grow and evolve is vital to your sense of well-being and your legacy. Remember, others are watching and taking notes. You take the risks and move forward which gives others permission. Within you is an infinitely deep pool of limitless abundance and universal wealth. Being willing to take just one cup of this limitless bounty is a game changer for you. Go for it!

In summary, your legacy has within it service, commitment to the greater good and a sense of completeness. Allow your vision and inner promptings to emerge through your intellect, emotions, physicality, and spirituality. Maintain a peer group of like-minded explorers. These connections offer the fertile ground for your transformation. Whether your spiritual pursuit is active or not at this moment, be open, be receptive, and respond to any promptings you receive. Allow your authentic heart's desire to come forth and brighten the world.

Points to Ponder:

1. What is legacy?

2. What legacy do you want to leave behind?

3. What is spirituality to you?

4. How do you connect spiritually?

5. How do you know you are a seeker?

6. What are you most curious about learning?

CONCLUSION

Being intensely sensitive in an often chaotic and insensitive world can be challenging and often tricky. Fortunately, there are increasing numbers of people coming forward while honoring their sensitive and spiritually connected nature.

Bringing together your intensities, gifted uniqueness, and your spiritual sensitivities is a powerful trifecta that offers a light of Hope to our world. You, my friend, are here on purpose with a mighty purpose to live and be your authentic, sovereign self. Your purpose encompasses much more than work, it is your authentic presence that brings you ultimate fulfillment while being a beneficial presence.

By taking your unique qualities and bringing them into our society in meaningful ways, while growing and evolving in your understanding and expression, you offer the generations to come a guiding light. It can be difficult to come out of your intellect long enough to listen to your innermost knowingness. It is worth the effort and investment. It is the harmony of linear and nonlinear intelligence that has a beautiful synergistic impact.

When you choose to expand from an inner locus of control, adversarial actions of others have no place to land. You, then become the living representation of inner harmony and inner peace. Every time you focus outward or run into your head to "figure it out", you miss the mark of your true genius by discounting a vital part of who you are.

I hope this book has offered you inspiration, perspective, support, and encouragement to live your most authentic life with an inner integrity. I see you. I support you.

In invite you to join the *Someone Gets Me* group to share with others of like mind and essence.
www.facebook.com/groups/someonegetsme

Appendix

Are You Intensely Sensitive?
Take this Quiz and See!

These are all Yes or No questions. If you think, "Well, sometimes or maybe" then the answer is a yes!

1. When you become interested in something new, you go "all in" and learn as much as you can.

2. You seem to be more sentimental than your family or friends, often becoming teary eyed or passionate about a topic with more animation than others.

3. People often tell you to calm down and not be so intense when you "get going".

4. You seem to "know" the answers to questions and challenges without always knowing how you know.

5. Certain fabrics and tags in clothing are unbearable, not simply uncomfortable.

6. When many things are happening, you become easily distracted then frustrated.

7. It is often difficult to fall asleep because you can't stop thinking about solutions and creations.

8. When you are busy, you tend to move as if with blinders on and others have told you to slow down and be more social which is perplexing because you "are just getting things done."

9. Small talk and seemingly superficial talk are boring or useless and you typically avoid it if you can.

10. Your heart hurts when you are listening or watching someone in pain.

11. You are a visionary and struggle with the day-to-day routines of getting things done.

12. You are a time optimist: You think you can get things done much faster than in reality; and/or your sense of time seems skewed from others in your life.

13. You become overwhelmed easier than others when there is a lot of stimuli including loud noise, too much background interference or distractions.

14. You have bouts of existential depression or loneliness when you look around and wonder where the people are who will understand or "get" you.

15. You have pretended to not be as smart or creative as you are to fit in within a situation.

16. Self-doubt and performance anxiety are things you must deal with.

17. You use complicated syntax in writing and speaking. Examples includes frequent commas and semicolons.

18. Your sense of humor is not easily understood by others.

19. You often use more varied vocabulary than many others.

20. You either act before thinking or over think which gets in the way of your decisions and outcomes.

21. You have wondered if you were an impostor or a fraud at times in your school or work life.

22. You have an on/off switch and there seems to be little middle ground.

If you scored more than 11 to 15 "Yes" responses, then you are moderately intensely sensitive**.

If you scored more than 16 or more "Yes" responses, then you are extremely intensely sensitive**.

* Intense Sensitivity refers to being gifted with overexcitabilities (intensity) coupled with a spiritual sensitivity (empath, strong intuition)

GLOSSARY OF TERMS

5 Essentials – As described in my book *Where Do You Fit In?* These are essential gifts that are important aspects to your nature and way of engaging with the world.

Creator – The Source of all that is in the Universe. Intended to reflect the vastness and possibilities in life rather than a particular worldview.

Dabrowski - Kazimierz Dąbrowski was a Polish psychologist, psychiatrist, and physician. Dąbrowski's posited association between overexcitabilities and giftedness appears to be supported in other research studies. For more information about Dabrowski and his work, you can start here: https://www.sengifted.org/post/overexcitability-and-the-gifted

Empath Distress Disorder – A term I use to describe the constellation of maladies that can appear in sensitive, empathic individuals. Symptoms include anxiety, sleep difficulties, stomach problems, malaise and more.

Empathy – The inherent ability to understand another's experience as if it were being experienced by the self. Being able to intimately "feel" another's emotion.

Fundamental Principles – This represents the spiritual principles that underlie our world. These principles include kindness, compassion, strength, love, faith, life, elimination, zeal, order, wisdom and more.

Gifted – An individual who evidences high achievement capability in such areas as intellectual, creative, artistic, or leadership capacity, or in specific academic fields, and who may need services or activities not ordinarily provided to fully develop those capabilities in academic, family and professional settings.

Good – Capitalized words reflect the spiritual principle rather than the secular definition. The spiritual principle of the Good reflects the highest form of a thought, word, action, or item. It is the ideal.

Higher Principles – See Fundamental Principles

Highly Sensitive Person – A term brought forth by Elaine Aron in the 1990's. A highly sensitive person (HSP) is often a neurodivergent individual who is thought to have an increased or deeper central nervous system sensitivity. The person may or may not be gifted.

Integrity Within – A person who is aligned in mind, heart, and gut/soul. Inner alignment yields inner integrity.

Intensely Sensitive Person – An individual who has both overexcitabilities and spiritual sensitivities in the form empathy and intuition.

Intuition -The highest form of intelligence is used by many visionaries in making discoveries and decisions. It comes in many forms with varying degrees of sensitivity and messaging.

Legacy – What you leave behind for the generations to come as they navigate their lives. I try to think 7 generations in the future when making major decisions.

Neurodiversity – The term referencing an individual who processes their world in a way that differs from the norm of common society. Often, special accommodations to deal with the tangible world are helpful.

Overexcitabilities – A term coined by Kazimierz Dabrowski. Common in gifted individuals that play a prominent role in Intense Sensitivities.

Source – See Creator

Twice Exceptional - Referencing individuals who are both gifted and have another characteristic like ADD, Depression, Anxiety, or the like.

ABOUT THE AUTHOR

Dianne A. Allen, MA is an intuitive mentor, speaker, author, ambassador, hope agent and life catalyst. Dianne has been involved in personal and professional development as well as mental health and addiction counseling during her several decade career. She creates exciting and diverse experiences for people to navigate life's setbacks and allow their unique vision to emerge.

Dianne inspires people in personal transformation through thought provoking services from speaking and podcasting to individual intuitive mentoring and more. She uses her years of experience coupled with years of formal education to blend powerful, practical, and effective strategies and tools for success and satisfaction.

Dianne hosts the *Someone Gets Me* podcast that aims to inspire listeners to say yes to their vision through powerful interviews and solo shows stemming from requests and questions being asked by clients, colleagues, and listeners.

She has authored: *How to Quit Anything in 5 Simple Steps - Break the Chains that Bind You, The Loneliness Cure, A Guide to Contentment, 7 Simple Steps to Get Back on track and Live the Life You Envision, Daily Meditations for Visionary Leaders, Hope Realized,* and *Where Do You Fit In?*

As CEO and Founder of Visions Applied, Dianne dedicates her time and talent to working with people who want to live their heart's desire and want expert guidance and support. Dianne enthusiastically joins with her clients to engage in an enhanced life's vision.

Connect with Dianne:

- www.visionsapplied.com

- www.msdianneallen.com

- www.linkedin.com/in/dianneallen

Someone
GETS ME

How Smart and Intensely Sensitive People Can
Thrive in an Insensitive World

www.ingramcontent.com/pod-product-compliance
Lightning Source LLC
Chambersburg PA
CBHW031154020426
42333CB00013B/662